W9-ABJ-377

Spiritual Dimensions...

Spiritual Dimensions in Teaching High School Religion

by
Sr. M. Michael Doherty, IHM

ALBA · HOUSE   NEW · YORK

SOCIETY OF ST. PAUL, 2187 VICTORY BLVD., STATEN ISLAND, NEW YORK 10314

Library of Congress Cataloging in Publication Data

Doherty, Mary Michael
    Spiritual dimensions in teaching high school religion.
    1.   Christian education of young people.
    2.   Catholic Church—Education.   I.   Title.
    BV1485 . D65   377' . 8'2   76-908
    ISBN   0-8189-0328-7

Nihil Obstat:
Daniel V. Flynn, J.C.D.
Censor Librorum

Imprimatur:
✠ James P. Mahoney, D.D.
Vicar General, Archdiocese of New York
January 21, 1976

*Designed, printed and bound in the United States of
America by the Fathers and Brothers of the Society of St. Paul,
2187 Victory Boulevard, Staten Island, New York, 10314,
as part of their communications apostolate.*

1 2 3 4 5 6 7 8 9 (Current Printing: first digit).

TABLE OF CONTENTS

INTRODUCTION

Communicating the Christian message to youth today requires different yet effective direction in the educational methods followed. Those techniques that were successful at another age are being replaced by the involvement of students in programs contributing to their spiritual formation. *To Teach as Jesus Did*,[1] and the other proclamations of the Bishops of the United States that have been issued since Vatican II offer ideas and directives that contribute to the spiritual development of adolescents in keeping with their longings in their search for God.

Reaching out through activities offers students those religious experiences that contribute to their growth as Christians. These pilot studies require that teachers have an understanding of the psychology of learning in order to be effective in making Christ real and personal in the hearts of their students. For this reason, ongoing inservice seminars provide religious educators with varying types of programs that will challenge students to live as Christian witnesses. No teaching of religion will change, unless the teachers are exposed to the objectives, values, attitudes, and techniques that alert teachers to the psychological principles that will vitalize their teaching.

The Christian community is the very heart of Catholic education and this concept must be taught and lived. Christ established the idea of a Christian community when He gave men the commandment to love one another. To live in community, one must develop a wholesome self-image. Many fail in life because they do not acquire that intelligent self-concept which gives them greater self-confidence, which enables them to live in keeping with the teachings of Christ.

Students need to have experiences in the prayer groups which are increasing in numbers today. Experiments reflect that the classroom is an ideal place to present such programs which are an outgrowth of various spiritual movements. Inspirational teaching enables youth to become involved in different types of prayer, such as Scripture reading, meditation, and spontaneous prayer in the form of praise and thanksgiving.

Closely allied to the development of prayer groups among teen-agers is the evangelization or youth ministries which offer students different approaches for studying their religion in this age when the peer cult dominates. This movement is reflected in the publications of the activities of those of other faiths who are active on high school and college campuses as noted in Teen Challenge, the Crusades for Christ and youth rallies. Catholic educators could adapt the teaching of religion to the apostolic zeal of their students as they offer new avenues within the many activities of the youth ministry that will enable them to proclaim the Gospel message.

With emphasis upon the development of the spiritual dimensions of young adults, Catholic educators need to re-examine that call to discipleship with Christ, those commitments which are for a short time, or that complete consecration for a life time. The study of the vocation of man is being considered within the religious program after being neglected for the last decade.

Since man learns from imitation, the in-depth study of these people who have made an impact upon contemporary times will contribute to the spiritual life style of youth through these movements which have provided programs on prayer, contemplation, retreats, and days of recollection. Selecting the biographies or autobiographies of Pope John XXIII, Mother Theresa of Calcutta, Thomas Merton, Thomas Dooley, Mother Seton, and comparable people and assigning them to students, using the seminar approach in teaching, will inspire generous souls to consider the part they must play in bringing Christ to others.

This program of electives considers the spiritual formation of youth, yet the teaching of doctrine has not been neglected. The activities are intended to vitalize teachings of eternal truths which can not be taught in isolation. Values which are stressed today become part of the offerings as students are encouraged to make self-evaluations that they might relate these learning experiences to Christian living as opposed to completing assignments.

Teachers become consultants in these programs, not the hearers of recitations. The classroom is a laboratory where students work during class time to share the findings later. Individualized instruction is encouraged as students are motivated to choose the assignments in which they want to become involved. All recommendations are intended as creative ideas with directives that can be adapted to different needs and interests in keeping with the objectives.

Catholic educators will find within these programs student-orientated involvements which will enable youth to meet the needs of these contemporary times. They will indeed be trained to spread the Good News of Christ through the different activities in which they have been involved in the varying apostolates.

—SISTER M. MICHAEL, IHM

February 1, 1975

1. The entire book follows the proclamations of the Bishops which have been published during the last decade and includes *To Teach as Jesus Did. Basic Teachings of the Catholic Religion,* and the *General Catholic Directory* which continues to be revised. All are published by the Bishops of the United States and can be secured from United States Catholic Conference, 1312 Mass. Ave., Washington, D.C. 20005.

Spiritual Dimensions...

CHAPTER ONE

INSERVICE SEMINARS ACTIVATE RELIGION TEACHERS

Through orientation seminars, teachers will be activated in the new dimensions for presenting religion. They will create that climate for learning that will enable youth to participate in the religious experiences suggested. The teachers of religion must change their attitudes, techniques, and approaches in directing teenagers toward Christ. The ways of yesterday that were so successful, must be replaced by the demands of today, which can be effective, if understood. Yet, the great work accomplished by religion teachers of other decades should not be overlooked. Dedicated religious nurtured the faith as they educated millions in the teachings of Christ during the past generations. Students were different and the times were different. In keeping with the instructional procedures of those particular eras, they kept the faith alive and vibrant. They were excellent educators. As leaders they were resourceful and had a remarkable influence in building the Church in America.

Stress the Spiritual

These inservice seminars are the very heart of developing effective teaching. Youth must be formed in keeping with the spiritual dimensions which are being stressed at this time. Basic doctrines and religious values are not replaced. They become an integral part of this emphasis upon renewal in Christ. Though the religion teacher enters the classroom with advanced degrees, she must be active in the on-going seminars in order to adapt her teaching to the changes that are taking place. As teachers vitalize their teaching, they inspire and motivate students who hunger for the spiritual. Through these inservice programs, teachers will incorporate within their religion classes of prayer and contemplation, a deeper knowledge of Scripture and of Christ so that youth will be prepared for the enrichment of their own spiritual life and for the youth ministries as they bring the Good News to others.

Teachers need to consider the problems that exist within society itself so that they can adapt the teaching of religion to the problems of today that religion might be related to *now* as asked for by students.

Problems Must Be Met

Social problems have alienated youth and encouraged the so-called generation gap because of the inconsistencies that they observed in what was said and what they observed in action. The factors that have contributed to the apathy and indifference of youth are to be found within society itself. As Catholic educators are aware of these concerns that have dominated these times they will be able to make the necessary changes especially in attitudes. As students come to understand what has brought about these differences and become aware of the importance of the love of Christ they will choose to follow His plan for them as they become involved in a program that makes such possible. Those problems to be considered are:

Estrangement from traditional values which have been so disturbing, for the actions of adults belie what they say, what they preach.

Feelings of unrest and indifference lead to uncertainty. Youth longs for a deeper meaning of being—for living.

Disenchantment with organized religion, (not with God, nor with the spiritual dimensions of life). There is a renewed interest in youth's longing for Christ.

Quest for authentic values that they have been deprived of with the emphasis on the present secularistic and materialistic ways for living. (*To Teach as Jesus Did*).

Teachers should consider these changes through an open-end discussion early in one of their inservice seminars. Illustrations would enable them to present religion for modern times. Students should be encouraged to give incidents that would confirm these changes and to give additional ones that they have experienced.

Growth in Technology

Allied to the problems related to society are the problems that have arisen from the advancement in technology. They, too, must be understood so that youth will be better able to cope with the changes that technology has brought throughout the entire world such as:

Greater material prosperity which has never been experienced before. This has contributed to much of the selfishness among men which is completely contrary to the Gospel teachings.

The gap between the rich and poor nations has been widened and proposes new threats to the dignity of man. This vast wealth of the richer nations must be shared with others as required by God in His plan.

Destruction of many smaller companies has accompanied this sudden growth in wealth by larger corporations at the expense of others. Such has destroyed stability, friendships, human values, and trust.

Greed, self-indulgence have increased, while eliminating love, faith, and hope which should dominate. This has contributed to uncertainty, fear, turbulence and destruction through war. (*To Teach as Jesus Did*).

This advancement in technology needs to be faced rather than feared. Youth needs to become aware of these problems with the conviction that they can change these present destructive evils. This is where the daily news enters the religion classroom and students see that the Gospel values require that they assume in this generation the responsibility for making changes. Motivated, they will learn how to make intelligent choices in the use of basic resources in keeping with the teachings of Christ.

Proclamations of the Bishops

In addition to the popular proclamation of the Bishops of the United States, *To Teach as Jesus Did,* there have been several others that should be read by each teacher of religion and a brief review should be shared with one another. They do not differ in content; rather they show the concerns of those responsible for the teachings of Christ when confusion arose shortly after the close of Vatican II. *The General Catechetical Directory,* approved by the Sacred Congregation of the Clergy, has gone through several editions by involving the laity and the priests in preparing a final document which will become the official program upon which to base the experimental studies that will continue for the next decade. This *Directory* will be a great asset to parents, teachers, and students and will bring about stability to the teaching of religion. It provides also for the varying teaching techniques that will involve youth so religion will become more meaningful to them.

Another document entitled *The Basic Teachings for Catholic Religious Education,* sponsored by the National Conference of Catholic Bishops, develops themes for further study which are related to the documents previously included. It should be reviewed by following the themes and in relation to the proclamations. The themes indicate what youth are concerned about: importance of prayer, participation in the Liturgy, Holy Scripture, witnessing to Christ, and the doctrines related to Salvation History, the Sacramental life, Mary, Christian community and living in union with God.

These recommendations of the bishops should be studied in

the light of the *Documents of Vatican II. The Church in Our Day* offers an excellent background for implementing change that would be enlightening if incorporated into the teaching of religion.

Enriching through Seminars for Inservice

With on-going inservice seminars, the teachers' intellectual and spiritual lives will be enriched, especially through the review of these proclamations which stress the informal approach as opposed to the traditional formal approach to the study of religion. Realize that the teaching process vitalizes the substance of the religion curriculum. The changes needed come from the concepts developed, as opposed to memorized facts. The emphasis placed on involvement in religion experiences enables youth to encounter Christ through the different suggested activities. Consider the following with the teachers in the light of the readings prepared by the Bishops which they should have completed:

Assign teachers to report on several chapters or from those chapters related to the particular study at one time. Determine how the suggestions given can be implemented at the different class levels.

Record these reviews and recommendations on cassettes so they can be used at other inservice seminars for the new teachers or so they will be available for teachers who would like to consider the details later.

Prepare directives that will be helpful for teachers and that will develop other ideas for teachers to involve their students.

Encourage the teachers to try different ways. Hold exchange ideas during a workshop so all can determine the effectiveness and values of varying ways of implementation.

Evaluate assignments with students. Listen to their recommendations and consider them at the inservice seminar so teachers can determine what should be changed.

Determine the different ways that students can be involved intelligently without wasting their time, and how these assignments will contribute to the deepening of their spiritual life.

Objectives

Teachers should be exposed to the objectives that provide the atmosphere for this renewed emphasis in relating Christ to their actual teaching. Then they can be developed with the students who need to know where they are going. These concrete objectives prepare the way as they enter into the involvement assignments.

In these seminars, the teachers could consider the objectives together to determine ways they could be implemented. Assign certain ones to students and require them in their own way to illustrate how they can make them meaningful. Through the sharing of the findings in each group, with both teachers and students, they could be covered in a few sessions. Some teachers might want to change them to behavior objectives as used in the other disciplines. They can be easily reworded to be presented as such. Review from time to time so that they will become an integral part of the learning process:

To know and love God and to realize God's great personal love which is too frequently missed unless presented in many ways. Explain how.

To understand moral values and to make them personal. How? To form right consciences without developing guilt complexes. Explain.

To learn how to make free and responsible decisions without following the crowd.

To be generous, to give of self, to make sacrifices in the service of others. List ways.

To live in keeping with Christian principles. What are they?

To develop your own personal goals by which you will live and influence others.

To foster your spiritual life through prayer, reading of Scriptures, following the sacramental life so that you will attain that union with God for which everyone hungers. Consider how.

To realize your apostolic responsibility to fulflll the mandate of Christ which is to proclaim the Good News, the mystery of salvation.

To live as Christian witnesses influencing others for good. That is what being a leader really means.

To know that you can change the world if you will.

Values incorporated

The important points will be vitalized as they are intelligently understood, and will in time become an integral part of the religion class, and the life style of the students. They are:

Make man's faith living, conscious, and active through the type of instruction presented.

Strive to relate human culture to the news of salvation as noted in Christ's teachings, especially the parables.

Organize religion classes with themes or religion experiences related to life and integrated in the light of faith.

Integrate religious truths and values with the type of life they are being prepared to live as modern apostles who assume responsibility for their own spiritual development and for presenting the teachings of the Gospels.

Orientate the teaching of religion to Christian service, to the formation of a community of faith, and to the commitment of youth to their particular ministries.

Include the authentic doctrines with a contemporary presentation so youth will participate in the religion program.

Provide the life style that enables teachers and students to live a life of prayer with Christ as reflected in the Gospel values.

Build within the religion classes a Christian community which will include students, parents, and teachers, as well as those they serve in different capacities.

Encourage programs that enable students, faculty, and at times their families to participate in the liturgical and paraliturgical activities that foster each one's spiritual life.

Stress the Gospel virtues taught by Christ such as peace, justice, love, patience, respect for life and for others, etc. This will deepen their concern for human needs.

Plan programs that will inspire youth to choose those areas of social, political, professional and economic life that will enable them to live the moral code in keeping with the teachings of the Church. Then the present destructive life styles are likely to be changed.

Develop with youth those competencies and skills that will make them effective leaders and thus influence for good because of these abilities.

Go over these objectives and values with the students as well as others that might be helpful in directing their learning activities. Have them explain their meaning and give ways they could be implemented so they could grow as persons and develop a deeper spiritual life. Conclude by requiring them to make resolutions by which they could live these values.

Psychological Principles

In the exchange of these psychological approaches necessary for the teaching of religion, teachers will suggest others that are of even greater value and will determine different ways to make these effective in the learning process. Some of the following relate to the psychological makeup of people rather than the psychological techniques and should be taken into consideration as teachers work in the formation of students:

Many changes have taken place in this fast moving world. Students can relate these to the changes within the church and in the teaching of religion if you ask them to list the changes in the different areas that they have observed. Consider how these changes are making a contribution to the future.

Working with students in small groups, do not allow those who dominate or are aggressive to deter others. Realize that people have certain hangups. Those who are over-aggressive are insecure and this is their means of escape.

If students are encouraged to act in a mature manner, they are able to respect those with strong reactions on certain subjects and re-direct their thinking to other facets of the same problem which need consideration.

Attention getting prevails among teenagers. Often youth take certain stands so that they will be recognized and become important. This could be a sub-conscious reaction, but the class should be made aware of their want of sincerity, that they are crying to be accepted, to be wanted, to be included, to be loved. These people must be listened to and directed towards assuming responsibilities within activities that will enable them to enjoy the importance for which they long.

Classes should begin with prayers, meditation, or a reading, etc., and students should take their turns in opening and closing classes in their own creative way. This should establish a relaxed atmosphere, especially if the teacher often introduces the class presentation with a story, an incident, a joke, even a cartoon. These different techniques hold the attention of students.

Since growth takes place in every encounter, be it an event, a person, an assignment, or a reading, these activities from which youth chooses to pursue further knowledge will contribute to their development and maturity.

Changes Challenge the Religion Curriculum

The chapters which follow await creative minds to implement them within the religion classroom. The suggestions made by the bishops in the varying documents encourage this informal atmosphere which accompanies the suggested activities that will vitalize the teaching of orthodox doctrine and the plans of Christ in the Gospels. They will challenge youth in the offerings of the religion curriculum which must be reviewed in these seminars. The programs could be:

Taught as complete electives in themselves. Or several of them could be combined and offered as one elective each semester.

Incorporated into the present electives within the religion curriculum, especially those that are related.

Become part of the vitalization of units of study offered for a semester or a year.

Selected in part to make more realistic certain assignments through the emphasis upon teaching religion concepts, rather than facts. Applications must be made to life through the religious experiences that involve the students.

Used in changing the attitudes of students toward learning religion. The objectives and goals are present with directives for participating in these religious experiences.

Related to leadership training which is essential if the youth ministry is to be encouraged, and lay evangelists will be prepared. Techniques for leadership training must be incorporated into the total program.

Offered by selecting parts and presenting what is called mini-courses so students will experience greater depth as they are exposed to these newer ideas in learning religion and making Christ more personal to them.

These suggestions lend themselves to study during the inservice seminar to determine what ideas to incorporate into their particular classes and how. The ideas that follow will include techniques in learning and integrating religious experiences within the religion curriculum.

Integrated Curriculum Develops the Complete Person

The curriculum offerings should integrate doctrine and values as related to life. Through this approach, one should develop as a complete person. The spiritual life deepens as youth are exposed to the consideration of contemporary trends, as studied in the Word. Youth will be motivated to make that complete commitment as they enter into the religious experiences offered in the Gospel teachings. The following will contribute to the development of students as they are involved in the curriculum organized:

To proclaim the Gospel message in the spirit of joy.

To read the Word frequently and to apply it to life.

To bring about social reform in keeping with Christlike values.

To live with hope and love in giving service to those in need.

To achieve personal relationships with Christ.

To realize that evil and sin exist. They must be overcome.

To not let defeat and despair destroy one.

To live with dignity as a person, and to respect life.

To bring about the development of Christian communities.

To participate in youth's ministry which is so attractive today.

To come to know the Holy Spirit and to call on Him.

To know and spread the basic doctrines of the faith.

To teach within the magisterium of the Church.

To become involved in programs that provide apostolic action.

To live one's faith with a new vision of God, of self, of the world.

Many of these directives are to be found in the varying electives which follow. Follow Christ's methods of teaching which are as modern as the latest text book. Christ taught using the idioms of His time. He reached the people as He went out to them through the parables which illustrated His message as He walked the earth.

In order to offer excellent programs in the religion curriculum so that the faith of youth will be vitalized, teachers need to keep in mind the supporting activities:

Use intelligently the religion materials in the form of books, pamphlets, tapes, films, film strips, that will provide these experiences. Train students to use machines.

Have teachers attend professional programs that offer conferences on the formation of youth in the things of Christ, on how to live their faith, and how to encourage the development of active apostles.

Introduce team teaching. This will demand cooperative planning so these changing attitudes will become part of the curriculum in both offerings and methods of teaching.

Make use of student teacher assistants and student teacher aides who will prepare the materials and direct some of the activities.

Work with the parishes and other groups, especially if you have included in the curriculum that once-a-week religion training program so students will be prepared to teach religion in their own parishes.

Curriculum Contributes to the Formation of Youth

The curriculum offers definite content that is different, and encourages methods of teaching that vary from the traditional. Its flexibility should direct students toward Christ as the teacher offers opportunities that will encourage them:

To develop educated consciences according to the tenets of Christ.

To live with personal convictions so they will be prepared to make their own contributions to this world.

To accept the opportunities for involvement in organizing and preparing scriptural, liturgical, and paraliturgical celebrations.

To encourage self-discipline that they might respect themselves as persons.

To meditate daily on God's love so they will realize it and share it in loving service for others.

To find self-identity through their personal relationship with Christ and to find this longing for self-fulfillment in their growth in love and service.

To realize that God lives this moment in history.

To grow in trust and confidence that will contribute to the increase of faith within one, as well as to that longing for freedom and healthy independence which will become part of one as he realizes the importance of these qualities.

To deepen your personal relationships with others as you learn to accept those who are different, annoying, even hostile.

To know the attitudes that prevent youth from developing as they really could be, those weaknesses of character and personality such as extreme shyness, inferiority feelings, unnecessary fear that can dominate their decision and prevent them from taking that step of faith which is essential in order to participate in the religion programs that will make Christ more personal to students.

To draw conclusions, not to be easily swayed, to consider the facts; to think for one's self and not to follow the so-called "in" crowd.

To read and meditate on the Word of God. The Incarnate Christ is present now. He continues to reveal Himself as youth listens and hears Him in the Word.

To be God's instrument for His apostolic work as carried out by man.

Through these built-in formation activities students will grow in positive ideals and constructive attitudes as created in this climate of learning such as to:

Locate materials which give them varying viewpoints.

Learn the many references available and use them.

Be able to interview people to determine their opinions.

Read widely from books other than texts. Make own bibliographies.

Enter into discussions intelligently, respecting others opinions.

Use time to advantage; grow in independent study on their own.

Be articulate and convincing in communicating and sharing ideas.

See relations and make application to modern life here and now.

Psychological Orientation

In order to present the content of religion in any form, students must be prepared for this psychological orientation which will involve them in the learning process. Through illustrations in the inservice seminar, teachers will become aware of these techniques that make such orientation possible as they review the meaningful experiences which they should include in their week-to-week presentation:

Assignments should grow out of the program which has been presented and not be given in order to cover so many questions, or pages.

Audio visual materials should not be over-used. Students must be prepared for the purpose of the presentation so that they will be effective in giving them the message intended.

Generalizations come in many forms such as myths or half truths. This should be pointed out so students would not preface their remarks with: you know, someone said, everyone says, I heard, everyone thinks, people believe, they say, etc. Demand verification and confirmation of the presentations that are doubtful. Then students will learn to be more careful.

Assignments require guidelines and directives so students can choose activities within the total study program which will require different readings, plans, preparation, study techniques, ways of sharing, review, and involvements. Be sure to allow time in class for preparation. Every meeting does not have to be a recitation.

Learning experiences should be so planned that they do not always have to be written. Youth are bored by written questions and answers and memorizing facts. This approach based on involvement should include assignments that will: require students to watch TV, a film, a news report and relate to the religion class at that time, to review books enthusiastically for the book club or group, without having to write a book report, give intelligent oral reports, present findings by following good discussion techniques, or participating in dialogue, panel, or open-ended discussions.

Differ Teaching Techniques

Changes in attitudes through activated teaching techniques while keeping basic doctrines are more likely to offset the destructive evils and should enable man to live as God asks of him in these times. These approaches, if correctly understood and applied, should make Christ more personal to the youth who hunger for the spiritual. They must live with faith and grow in that faith through these experiences in which they will be involved.

In the recommendations made in *To Teach as Jesus Did*, Catholic educators were encouraged:

To experiment with pilot studies which would be offered in different religion programs.

To evaluate these creative ideas and to offer teachers innovative techniques for teaching.

To offer programs that enable youth to live as Catholics even in the instability of these times.

To continue to search for other forms that will make youth live their commitment to the faith with a sense of values.

To stress programs that will contribute to the formation of youth without omitting basic doctrines so they will establish a faith community in keeping with the purpose of the sacraments of baptism and confirmation which they have received.

To listen to and be sensitive to the problems and questions that trouble youth.

To share ideas, plans, programs and evaluations with other faculty members so that the goals of the school and the particular class will bring about the unity that makes possible further pilot studies.

As teachers share the different ways they make these and other ideas part of their teaching, they will realize how involved their students are in learning their religion and enjoying the experiences that contribute to their growth as Catholics. Evaluation is essential if teaching is to be effective in any discipline and for that reason the term accountability is stressed at this time in the teaching-learning process.

Chairman of Department Coordinates Seminars

The chairman of the religion department is responsible for organizing these inservice seminars. She could work with the coordinators of each class and they should assume responsibility for the different activities, especially at their class level. Together they need to:

Suggest and provide readings, materials, and activities that would be helpful. Maintain a faculty bulletin board to post especially the brochures that come from publishing companies so teachers will be aware of all that is available in the teaching of religion.

Consider with the teachers professional attitudes and principles that will enable them to create this informal atmosphere within the religion classroom as they prepare youth for these encounters with Christ and others.

Present demonstrations on how to bring about these changes, especially when teachers find it difficult to change to these newer approaches which can be more effective.

Prepare reading lists for the required books that should be read at each class level and the resource materials that could be used as related to the units of study.

Reevaluate the text books used, the electives offered, and make recommendations for changes in the teaching or the content, and also the supplementary materials.

Make available AV materials that could be used.

Assign faculty members different responsibilities in keeping with their abilities and interests so that all will be involved in the professional growth that will make the teaching of religion the heart of the total school program.

Provide time for these inservice seminars so that teachers will be able to participate.

Since youth longs for the spiritual, this phase of the religion program should be developed so both teachers and students will have these opportunities right on campus. Evenings of recollection for small groups should be available. Students could help organize. Sometimes their parents could be invited. There are so many ways retreats are conducted today that people enjoy and it is not unusual to participate in them more than once a year. Some other spiritual activities that could be offered are:

To provide daily Mass, or a set time to receive Holy Communion each day. Encourage daily visits to the Blessed Sacrament so youth will come to know the Eucharistic Christ.

To develop prayer groups and Scripture groups which students themselves generally will start or ask for.

To have mother-daughter retreats or masses, or father-son retreats or masses sponsored by a campus club or organization.

To hold a procession in honor of our Lady following the Lourdes' plan in the evening with lighted candles which could be a family affair.

To dedicate the entire school early in the year to the Sacred Heart of Jesus, and in October to the Immaculate Heart of Mary. Explain these devotions. They could take place during the regular school time, or at a parents' meeting so families would consecrate their homes also.

To offer communal penance services, or Scripture Services in preparation for a particular feast day.

To conduct a film festival related to the needs of these times, such as poverty, urban renewal, etc.

Religious Affairs Council for Students

Students want and are encouraged to work with teachers in the entire school program. Faculty members would find very helpful a Student Religion Council who could meet and even sit in some of these seminars to help with promoting the many programs that will demand the involvement of the entire student body. Two students could be elected from each class to the council. The chairman could be appointed or elected. Definite responsibilities could be listed so they could actively participate in promoting the religious activities on campus. They will need leadership training which should be provided if they are to be effective. Students should be motivated and inspired to choose these involvements. They should never be forced. Members of the council or other students should have charge of the publicity so all students will be aware of what is happening.

The student council will assist with planning many of the activities with the different classes. The teachers should delegate responsibilities and must work along with the students rather than giving them assignments. They need to be trained in how to assume responsibilities and how to motivate other students to become involved. Only through participation will leaders be trained and students formed.

The chairman of the religion council should also be a member of the student council which would integrate religion into the entire school program. He could be encouraged to present programs, ideas, or activities to the religion department seminars in order to seek the assistance of the faculty in promoting approved suggestions.

Students as Teacher Assistants

With this more flexible curriculum, teachers need more assistance in locating and preparing the materials for the class to use. They can be helped by those students who are willing to volunteer their services and accept the responsibilities required. Those who become involved are being trained as leaders and will grow in confidence and security which will make them effective in directing the activities of different members of the class. This will take time and no student should be given an assignment unless trained. A teacher with a particular ability for the psychological formation could conduct several seminars for all teacher assistants, and the routine activities should be the particular work of the teacher that the student is going to aid. The psychological experiences that need explanation are:

To learn human relations as they work with people and consider their sensitivities and hostilities.

To develop their own latent abilities as they grow in confidence in themselves.

To observe the different ways people attack problems, work with others, arrive at conclusions, and direct them accordingly.

To participate in those programs that will be enriching to a degree. They have talents such as art, drama, music, singing, etc.

To be exposed to all the varying techniques of learning such as drill, review, summarizing, outlining, discussion, speaking aloud, reading comprehension, etc., so they can help those who are slow.

To be able to review with the class the fundamentals of the basic doctrines so they will not be overlooked as students enter into more creative activities.

To set up the audio visual equipment and assist students in using same.

Once the assistant student teachers have been trained in the activities of class management, they should assume responsibility for each assignment. The regular teacher might have to supervise at first so errors will be prevented. Here are some ways the assistant can help:

To take the roll each day.

To start and end the class for the teacher in keeping with what is expected.

To keep a list of the activities or assignments so they can be checked off when completed or will be available for students who are absent. Give these assignments to them when they return.

To record all home work or other types of assignments. Keep a card on each student with a brief explanation. It should be helpful for the teacher to determine grades from such. Record all grades.

To assume responsibility for the order of the books, the distribution of papers, the collecting of assignments, filing papers, student folders if used, order within the room.

To see that the bulletin boards are attractive, related to the class, and changed frequently.

To explain to the class the use of the materials, guidelines, books, and directives distributed.

To work with individuals and small groups when preparing materials.

To use all AV equipment and have each ready when it is to be used in class.

To accompany small groups to the library, to the chapel for a service, on a field trip, or to another class where interdiscipline programs are being carried out.

To learn how to introduce and thank guest speakers and to involve students in asking intelligent questions as they participate.

To assist with planning assignments. Listen to students and make recommendations that will help them. Evaluate programs, books, assignments.

To select hymns, direct the singing, play the guitar if possible and prepare the songs by duplicating words.

Students must be trained to play their part as active lay leaders in the church of tomorrow. They must be involved in activating assignments as recommended by the pastoral messages of the Bishops. Then they will more likely assume personal responsibility for their own spiritual development.

To meet these immediate needs, Catholic schools must provide orientation classes within their inservice programs for the religion faculty that are not too time consuming. They need to be exposed to techniques that will professionally prepare them for the changes in attitudes and that will enable them to place emphasis upon religious experiences that will be effective. An on-going program at each class level directed by the religious coordinator will make such possible. The exchange of ideas that come from readings on the many experimental programs will bring about these changes. These once-a-week conferences will embody directives and will be accompanied by evaluation procedures that will direct teachers in offering more dynamic challenges.

Religion curriculum ideas provide Catholic educators with ways to incorporate programs into present courses, electives, or units of study without radical changes which are too frequently most discouraging because of the apparent demands made on the present teaching methods. The purpose is to integrate doctrine with values through the spiritual formation programs so that students will grow in this personal relationship with Christ.

CHAPTER TWO

CREATING A COMMUNITY OF FAITH

Conditions today prevent people from knowing one another, or living as neighbors, be it in the inner city, in apartments, or in the suburbs. The deep roots established in earlier generations, when people lived for decades in the same town or city, no longer exist. Notwithstanding this, Communities of Faith are arising in parishes spontaneously. Meeting a need, they develop in different ways. Though still in the transitional stage, they are important in that they contribute to the activating of one's faith. They take on many forms, from developing a faith-filled spirit within a class or a school, to the more radical small groups where young adults embrace poverty as they live in loving service for others.

These communities cannot be forced, yet the spirit which they encourage should enter into the religion classes and students should be exposed to the different types that are growing. Young families feel called by Christ in increasing numbers to live this life of sacrifice. College graduates who have experienced success in their professions or businesses have been leaders in establishing these Christian communities.

The most popular of these faith communities are small prayer groups or Scripture study seminars which are increasing in numbers. They meet frequently and share their religious experiences as they try to grow spiritually. Each community takes on its own identity, chooses a name, and sponsors some form of apostolic work, or its members are involved in different forms of service.

Regional meetings offer a supportive structure with opportunities to exchange ideas.

Contemporary readings on these religion experiences enable Catholic educators to adapt some of the ideas to the teaching of religion. True, during this experimental period, there might be offered programs that lack substance, that "turn on" youth, but not for long because they are so superficial. This is to be expected in any transition period. With frequent evaluation, such will soon end, for students are looking for programs with real values, that are genuine and not phoney.

Without a doubt, these seminars sponsored by Christian communities bring people back to God and His teaching. They come to know Him in a more personal way through these varying encounters. The newer proclamations on the teaching of religion recommend that youth be trained to live the gospels as they work and pray out of love together. The implementation of these experimental studies in keeping with the theology of Vatican II offers youth a new and different religion curriculum. This is their call to commitment in keeping with their baptism as Catholics and the promises made at the reception of confirmation. In this way they will identify with Christ and find the fulfillment for which they claim they long.

Spiritual formation must be attractive, active, deep, intense, and be present in different ways, not under pressure but with inspiration and conviction. Faith must be vitalized and youth must assume responsibility for their own development as persons, and as Christians. Students must understand Christ's message, live their Christian values, accept God's providence, and give in loving service which is asked from those given the gift of faith. Students will come to know Christ more intimately through these programs that involve them, especially with the emphasis upon the study of Scripture and prayer.

Creating Christian Communities within Our Catholic Schools

Youth have to be involved in these experiences that will make religious truth and values part of daily living. Faith is on-going, a gift from God, that has to be nourished in different ways, and continually. A community of faith, as an integral part of the total teaching-learning process, is based upon the Catholic philosophy of education. Basic concepts, and not mere facts, must be estab lished that will provide the needed understanding to develop the faith of these young adults.

Concepts need to be developed. Each concept must be applied to the lives of students here and now. Concrete illustrations need to be considered so that these teenagers will understand the meaning of religion as intended by God. The class could suggest many ways of making these concepts concrete realities:

Christians are persons, pilgrims in time walking towards eternity for they are children of God and heirs of heaven. The several concepts included must become the very heart of their realization of why they are here and what they do.

As Christian students they should work to reach their potential in keeping with their particular abilities and talents. Let them give the different ways this can be accomplished, and how their attitudes could be changed if they are indifferent or apathetic.

Youth must strive to develop a complete personality as opposed to the fragmentary one, which is so destructive as found in unhappy lives, the increase of divorce, etc. Study in the light of the needed virtues.

Young adults should consider the ways they can incorporate the Gospel values into their lives through reading Scripture, reflecting and meditating on what Christ says to each one.

Catholics receive the Sacraments frequently. Such needs preparation to avoid the routine and the casual ways the sacraments are approached.

Christian Witnesses will influence for good. All the ways they could be involved should be illustrated.

Apostolic youth must bring the Good News to other people. Discover together the many ways they could be involved in doing this now.

People have a mission in life that can be filled by no other. Consider the different missions where they could serve.

Through the sharing of these findings on conceptual understanding, students will be prepared for the involvement activities that will make these concepts more meaningful.

Involvement Experiences

Conceptual learning requires process teaching. Students are always on the way, changing and growing, never completely arriving. Incorporate involvement activities to enable youth to grow through experiences such as:

Going out to people which will give them confidence in self.

Being trusted and accepted which enables them to assume responsibility for any assignment.

Giving of self in time, in the effort needed in order to accomplish a program or activity.

Offering to do volunteer work and to be consistent in seeing it through to the end.

In attacking problems with serenity and peace out of love.

The techniques that enter into these activities must be made meaningful so they offer students enriching experiences. Inspirational talks, suggested readings, student panels and reports will create the atmosphere that will change the classroom and thus create that community of faith. Have students finalize the understanding of the community of faith by implementing the following suggestions that need to be considered and clarified:

Give illustrations of what the community of faith means to you in keeping with the readings given.

What changes do you think the activities incorporated into this program would make in a religion classroom? Of what value are the suggested activities that will involve students, as opposed to regular religion assignments?

What on-going programs would you recommend from your readings that will develop a Christian community within the school, this classroom, your parish?

How do you think you could vitalize your own personal faith by reading Scripture and praying so that Christ will become personal to you?

What suggestions would you share with your family so that it could become more Catholic? What about family prayer, family devotions in keeping with the liturgical year? Do they help form a community within the family? What about the place of the Sacred Heart, the Blessed Virgin in the modern home? How could you read Scripture with your family? Have you tried? What happened?

What suggestions would you make to your parents that would help them to live their Catholic faith if they have become careless?

What programs should the school offer to help parents in keeping their homes Catholic as requested in Vatican II?

Make a list of things where parents could be helped in these confused times so they will want to live the Catholic faith more deeply.

Secularism in Catholic Homes

Serious consideration should be given to the decline of faith within Catholic homes which often are Catholic in name only. Different forms of secularism enter many a Catholic life. Think through the materialism that dominates as Christians are exploited on every level especially through advertising and TV recommendations as a way to live. Students need intelligent principles upon which to make decisions so they will not be swept away by the crowd motivated by secularistic attitudes. For discussion:

Permissiveness which is to be found in homes, in schools, in society, and which is difficult to cope with. Give examples.

Freedom about which people talk, and yet freedom is not free. It comes with a price, even a sacrifice. It is related to our democracy and to the total world picture with the threat of wars on many fronts and the sufferings which accompany same. Illustrate.

Over population is not *the* problem. Hunger is the basic problem today. The need is for creative minds to develop ways to increase the food supply of the entire world.

Birth control, abortion, divorce, and their accompanying evils such as trial marriages, pre-marriage experiences and other moral problems that destroy Christians as well as the evils of Communism that are spreading so rapidly. Relate to secularism.

Attitudes towards the poor, refugees, welfare, prisons, slums, the need for low income houses, care for senior citizens, medical help, the over use of drugs, drinking, popular magazines that are obscene as are some films and TV programs. What could be done?

Recommendations on what could change these problems should be determined so that youth will be able to cope with these destructive situations. Do not allow students to give mere opinion. They should be assigned articles to read that will give them information. Too frequently a religion class turns into a discussion session without the background research that would enable them to think on their own and evaluate what is being considered to make these changes.

Many other ideas cause defections. They should be considered in these open-end discussions. Consider them in the light of how they prevent people from living the fullness of their Christian life, especially in so-called Christian countries.

Closely allied to these moral problems are the personal reactions of students who must meet other social issues. The ways they think and react when they are confronted with ideas which are opposed to our Catholic teachings must enter into the formation of youth in keeping with the teachings of Christ. The psychological concepts that need direction are:

Following the crowd. Can they stand alone?

Making intelligent decisions, based on facts, not on feelings.
Acting on rumor, or "every one says," making generalizations.
Being decisive, confirming the facts of what has been reported
Making decisions on biases, prejudices, likes and dislikes.
Being apathetic and indifferent, not caring about problems.

The evaluations of their attitudes and reactions should alert them to the seriousness of the needed decisions if they are to really live their Catholic faith, and become the leaders to influence the world of tomorrow by bringing about some change.

Concepts of Community

Christian community must be intelligently and correctly understood before becoming involved in any activities. Too often, it is thought of as togetherness, that is, doing the same thing, at the same time, in the same way. Such a concept is wrong. The overstructure dominates, and does not allow that freedom of spirit which is essential. True, people will come together to share their different experiences but this should be more or less spontaneous. The Christian community is built on:

Sharing common beliefs and practices.
Participating in different forms of worship including the Liturgy.
Living with Christ-like goals, ideals, and values.
Surrendering self interests for the common good.
Accepting corporate responsibility.
Giving service out of loving concern.
Accepting the plans, ideas, and assistance of those within the community.
Using talents and abilities to develop this Christian community.

These ideas are not new. They must be re-vitalized within the religion classroom so that they will be considered in the parishes, organizations, and other groups who are involved in forming communities of faith. The directives will alert students to what is needed if the community is to last. The heart of every Christian community is the Mass and the Eucharist. Greater attention is being given to the attendance of Mass other than Sundays and, with the home Masses, devotion to the Holy Sacrifice is increasing. Through the frequent reception of Christ in Holy Communion there is more likely to be a more lasting union with the people and their many differences.

Different Types of Communities

In addition to studying the basic elements that enter into the founding of a faith community, students should be made aware that from the time of the apostles such have existed in parishes and organizations founded in the different ages, to care for the needs of other people. Together, the people grew spiritually, as they shared often on the person-to-person basis the abundance of their material resources. There has been a decline with time, due to the many changes that accompany this fast moving age. Now there is a return to communities that are different. They should be studied as students are given different Christian communities to report on. Then the class will be aware of what is going on in places other than their immediate circle. Here are a few, and there will be others that differ:

> Marriage Encounters, Cursillo programs.
> Charismatic groups that come in many types.
> Programs for the permanent deacons and their wives.
> CCD programs with the spiritual formation for the laity.
> The lay teachers in the Catholic schools and their spiritual inservice renewal programs.

Students could interview members of these different groups and report on their programs. They could attend any one of them. Most of them have on-going spiritual activities that could be included. Their personal reactions to what changes have taken place in their lives would be helpful in this study. They are likely to find some of them stronger in their spiritual formation than others. Directives accompany these activities that would offer information that youth could consider when they plan for their own type of spiritual involvement in any form of community. In addition to reporting on these movements that are well on their way, other students could select different groups to determine their plans:

Report on the parish prayer and Scripture groups. Tell how they came to be, what program they follow, how successful they are in contributing to the spiritual formation of the members, how they activate people to belong, etc. Visit the group or one of the leaders.

Study and report on Christian communities.

Require that every member of the class read the Acts of the Apostles and study them in detail to understand the earliest Christian communities. Consider also the religious communities that have existed for years and compare with the newer ones dominated by the laity.

Reflective readings, listening to tapes and songs, along with directives of the teacher will offer students ways to become members of a community as they become involved in experiences that enable them to:

Rediscover God in their lives, and there are many ways to do so.

Renew their dedication which is really their baptismal consecration.

Apply the Resurrection of Christ to their own resurrection which is to come.

Make their faith a real way of life which can be lived.

Participate in spreading God's Word.

The many ideas that are part of the religion curriculum will offer students programs in which they will become involved in developing different forms of faith communities within their religion class, within the school, in the organizations where they participate, in their parishes and in the communities where they are involved in service to people who need their talents.

Teachers must also incorporate into the class instruction attitudes and techniques that indirectly establish a Christian community. Such is impossible where students are allowed to be casual and careless because self-discipline is not demanded. An atmosphere that makes possible a community of faith can be created if instructors:

Demand excellence through the standards that must be met.

Encourage participation by giving students directives.

Develop potentials through motivation within the instruction.

Provide successful experiences through the guidelines.

Direct youth to meet frustrations and disappointments that arise.

Evaluating procedures will enable students to be responsible for their own development and prepare to be the leaders of tomorrow which the faith community would make possible. Certain readings from the documents would enable students to acquire the spirit of Vatican II which intends to lead them into the 21st century. These readings should accompany the varying pilot studies that the school sponsors.

Developing a Wholesome Self-Image

When youth are in search for identity and desire that self-fulfillment, they need to understand that they are identified with Christ through their baptism, and that through living the Christian life they can enjoy complete self-fulfillment. To enter intelligently into the newer religion programs where they assume responsibility they need to consider ways that will provide realistic experiences in understanding self. They must accept self and develop that wholesome self-image that will give them confidence to work with others. With positive attitudes towards self they are more likely to grow spiritually as they become leaders in these communities they choose to belong to and to contribute as Christian witnesses.

The activities that follow lend themselves to personal experiences that will assist youth in growing in this wholesome self-image. Students do not have to participate in each activity. They can choose those that they will enjoy and share with the class their findings. These varying considerations lend themselves to sophomores who have had a year of high school and understand to a degree where they are going and what they should accomplish. They are intended to make them aware of their responsibilities as students, as persons, as Christians, for some day they will have to give an account of their lives.

Evaluation Activities

To assist students to understand themselves, begin by having them evaluate themselves through questions so they can plan for their own future. The first series of questions could be used with the entire class. As the program continues, small discussion groups could determine ways to grow personally. The teacher needs to direct the thinking of the students so that they can reach the goals they have established in order to enjoy a wholesome self-image:

List your personal problems that you do not like, with which you are unable to cope. What are you doing about them? Where could you obtain help? You need not sign your name as these are personal to you.

List the problems you have observed among teenagers which reflect their want of a wholesome self-image. How do these prevent students from developing? Make suggestions on how attitudes could be changed, giving greater self-confidence.

How do high school boys and girls accept responsibility for their own self-development? Have you read books on personality? What recommendations did they make that are to be found in the Bible where Christ gave definite recommendations to grow in virtue?

Are you responsible for your own happiness? your own success? How is such possible? What about suffering? Why are there so many unhappy teenagers? unsuccessful ones? Why is suicide so high among young adults?

What qualities of mind and heart do you admire in a person? What ones do you dislike? Why? List the virtues that you think students should work on in their own development.

What do you do to develop your personality? Are you aware of this responsibility? Does the school neglect this phase of development? What would you recommend for your class? for you?

What recommendations would you make for people who are afraid, immature, are shy, withdrawn, aggressive, insecure? How would you implement each?

Do you know your potential as a person, as a student? Can you influence without being a leader, holding office? What are your strengths? weaknesses? What is the relationship of a good self-image to being a Christian witness?

How do you develop self-discipline? Is such possible or does it have to be part of the unseen structure that surrounds you? How do you grow in self-confidence? Give ways for each one of these needed qualities of mind and heart to become part of you so you will become an effective person, capable of assuming responsibility, through your own self-direction.

How do you handle failure that enters every life at some time? frustrations and disappointments? Do you blame others? What types of escape do you use? Give ways you can face reality.

The study of how to develop a wholesome self-image should contribute to your personal development if you have been open to what is related to teenagers in the journey through that turbulent period of formation within themselves. Many of these answers to questions will never be shared with others but they will open avenues to enriching experiences.

Developing Friends

A great problem in society today is loneliness, which is allied in many cases to alienation. Could this tragedy of loneliness, of feeling completely unwanted be avoided? Making and keeping friends are related to developing a wholesome self-image. In that so much in life depends upon personal relationships, a consideration of the following discussion questions might be worked on by another group during this time devoted to the study of personality:

Do you follow the crowd? Give illustrations of what youths do to be "in." Does the peer group dominate your life? Why? How? Can you stand on principles if the peer group does not approve?

Give ways you really love yourself, you accept others, go out to others that you do not like. Illustrate how you try to live joyously, creatively, positively, constructively. What suggestions would you make for implementing each one of these important qualities?

Are teenagers selfish as is claimed? What can be done about this selfishness? Show how they are also generous. List the different types of work in which they volunteer their services. Are they consistent? thoughtful of others? Do they expect too much from society?

Do teenagers make a contribution to the clubs they join? Why are they members only and do not share in the activities that demand service, offer a social life, and require spiritual growth?

Do you make friends easily? What is the real meaning of friendship? Where does loyalty come in? What is false loyalty? Explain what you have observed among so-called friends. Do you keep the friends you make?

Do you know the parents of your close friends? Do they

know your parents? Is this essential? Are your friendships confined just to school?

Should you confide in friends? To what degree? What about sharing family confidences, family problems? What is the value of having several friends as opposed to possessing one friend only?

Do you include others in your group, especially those who do not seem to belong? How could your class go out and include one or more in each of the groups that have naturally formed? Would this help?

Can you stand up to your friends when they want you to participate in what you know is wrong, in what your parents would not approve? Are you able to walk away and say "no" even at the price of losing them as friends?

Have you met so-called leaders among your friends or in your class that are impulsive, enter into things without thinking, without realizing the consequences?

What can be done about people who dominate, influence you and others and yet you do not want to be part of what they are doing? Confer with your parents how to handle them and several of the other problems that were included in this evaluation of making friends. They will have sound advice to give you even if you do not realize it right now. They can help you and guide you and save you from many heart aches. Begin with the first community of faith, your home. Going out to your parents will help that so called generation gap when you manifest trust in depending upon them for guidance in those things that matter.

These considerations, related to the development of the community of faith, will offer ideas which will make such possible, for it must begin in understanding and accepting self. The religion offerings should motivate youth so that spontaneously and naturally, without force, a community of faith will arise.

The emphasis is on the spiritual and personal formation of the students, for this is what they enjoy. The many discussions which have been suggested along with the readings will prepare the way. As they listen, make surveys, participate in programs, become acquainted with the many dynamic activities that youth of different faiths are involved in, they are indirectly being prepared to develop their own community of faith where growth in the things of God will come because of the atmosphere created.

CHAPTER THREE

REACHING OUT THROUGH RELIGIOUS EXPERIENCES

The term "religious experiences" can have several connotations. It is not to be considered as a peak religious action, a sudden conversion, a dramatic form of ecstasy, but do demand a total concentration of the whole person as opposed to the apathy and indifference which frequently accompany the studying of religion. The sameness day after day in listening to recitations of the exact material without application to life, or the lecture approach which is often boring, fail to involve students in the learning process, in appreciating the place of religion in their lives.

Climate for Religious Experiences

A climate of faith is created within the regular classroom where religious experiences are intelligently presented. They motivate the activities of the students. Religion teaching takes on a "faith look" as the daily experiences are seen in their relationship to life. They become alive and meaningful; they alert youth to transcendence within these experiences; they challenge contemporary assumptions and attitudes and vitalize the religious endeavors as they are communicated. To enter into these religious experiences, students must become present to themselves, aware of what they are doing and why.

Youth should learn to recall God's Presence as they study and work, as they call on Him to assist them and to walk with them wherever they will go. This Presence must become a reality to them. Then God's plan for each one of them unfolds itself as they become involved in the varying religion experiences. To the extent Christ becomes personal to these young adults will they grow and develop spiritually.

Catholic educators through pilot studies are providing programs that are enriching because of the spiritual activities that satisfy in different ways these longings for the things of God. These religious desires are not isolated to a few students. They are much more universal, as youth cry out for those activities that will enable them to activate and deepen their spiritual life.

In the many proclamations on the teaching of religion and especially in *To Teach as Jesus Did* will be found recommendations for different forms of religion programs that would replace the traditional ones of other years and explore new ways less formal and that could be adapted to the needs of youth. The recommendations that are made lend themselves to involve students in the programs that follow:

Youth need to be involved in varying forms of Christian service which will make their faith more meaningful as they meet the challenges of their Christian commitment.

Religious truths and values must be fully integrated in the light of faith. Programs must provide opportunities for observation, for association with other avenues of thought and previous learnings, and with the relationships of events and experiences that life provides in keeping with God's plan for them.

Youth must be exposed to the problems which face individuals and society now. Many of these experiences are oriented towards involvement assignments that contact people. There, they are likely to acquire those skills, virtues, and habits of heart and mind that will enable them to be effective in their faith communities.

Going out to people and being concerned about their needs reflect the Gospel values, develop a sense of responsibility, and prepare youth to be Christian witnesses, leaders of the Church of tomorrow where the laity will play such an important part.

Students must become aware of this Christ that they meet in Scripture and come to know Him personally. They must be steeped in prayer and have a deep sense of the Christian values that they are to bring to others.

The suggested activities which youth will be involved in through these pilot studies are experimental so are constantly being evaluated to determine their effectiveness.

Objectives for Reaching Out

The Youth Ministry offers programs that could be studied for its main thrust: to bring Christ and the Good News to others. This is the age of the youth cult and they have a definite status, as peers influence peers. People over 30 are less effective. They do not know what it is all about claims this younger generation. Catholic educators will note that in *To Teach as Jesus Did*, the writers gave consideration to the goals that lend themselves to the development of a youth ministry. These goals should be considered early in the religion class.

To face the problems that challenge today's youth, such as the increase of secularism in the thinking and acting of so many, and the decline of morals which are so destructive.

To act so that youth will be accepted by older people. The alienation and uncertainty that exists does not help them to develop as Catholics. There must be acceptance on both sides.

To make religion a vital part of life. Youth want to see the relationship of faith to daily living and it should be presented that way.

To provide those positively oriented experiences for which youth long in teaching religion rather than just using a text book.

To offset the disenchantment of youth with traditional religion from the way it has been taught and to present the essential content as Christ had intended.

To involve youth in the planning of their religious involvement experiences under the direction of a teacher who is open and willing to bring about change.

To enable youth to grow spiritually as they come to know Jesus because of their involvement in religious experiences where they study Scripture, grow in prayer, and are involved in music and songs which have so many messages just for them.

As students consider the pros and cons of these goals and determine ways they can be implemented they are more likely to become active participants in the mission of the church as they reach out to those who can benefit from what they have to offer. As they focus on action oriented activities they will exemplify what it means to be a Catholic for they will play a definite part in the varying communities where they serve. Youth needs direction in this apostolate and Catholic educators must provide the leadership and inspiration which will enable them to be co-workers in Christ's mission.

Activities for Reaching Out

So that youth will have a better understanding of the youth ministry in which they will be involved as presented in the many programs recommended in the different chapters, it would be worthwhile to prepare students by consideration of some of the following:

Visit any one of the teenage programs such as Teen Challenge. Some might like to read *The Cross and the Switchblade*, or *Run Baby Run*. These books open new avenues and offer definite challenges to their indifference to living a life of faith with confidence in God. Programs such as Youth for Christ are very popular and chapters are on high school and college campuses as well as in connection with different churches. Interview the people in charge of these organizations, the students who belong to them and find out what attracted them to become active and what they really do as Christians.

Two or three students could go together for these interviews and visits to these places.

Others could develop a resource center where the materials published could be displayed and made available for all members of the class. Contact ministers of the different religions and ask them for comparable materials that they use with their teen age groups that they are training directly or indirectly for the youth ministries. Through interviews and the published materials they will offer Catholic youth ideas and programs that they could adapt to the needs of the Church at this time. The dedication of these youth groups to the things of God is most edifying and inspirational.

Visit Christian Bookstores and note their publications. Report on same to the class and encourage others to see what they are doing to bring Christ to the world. Note also the name of the publishers. Many of them are publishing Catholic books.

Ask students to read *Newsweek, Time* and *US News and World Report* to note what they publish in their religion section; also observe that they devote an entire issue to some particular phases of religion. Save these copies for reference later.

Collect records or make cassettes of the popular songs with a message or the gospel songs which are to be found on radio or TV. Note the large number of small groups who come together, choose a name and are willing to sing for different organizations these songs related to Jesus and His mission in life. Students might develop their own groups and choose some of these songs to share as part of their youth ministry.

Send for sample copies of *Guide Post, Decision, Campus Life, Teen Challenge,* and comparable monthly publications. These publications are highly motivating in offering Catholic youth ideas in which they could become involved.

Some time should be given to the Youth Rallies in the early 70's. Materials are available from the organizations previously mentioned which will describe them in detail and offer leadership manuals that train those responsible for directing the activities.

The Catholic school is the center for the introduction of these religious activities. They might begin there, but should without too long of a delay become part of the religion programs sponsored by the parish so they could continue to be augmented long after students leave high school.

Enrichment through Religious Experiences

Students must come to appreciate the fact that they were made for greater things, that they pass this way but once and any good that they can do, they should, and that they possess God-given talents and abilities that must be developed to reach the potential as an educated Catholic with a definite commitment. The assignments that follow will assist students in realizing God's gifts to them as they become involved in reaching out to those who need them. These activities will enrich them personally. They could choose several of the suggestions and work in small groups. When completed they could present their findings to the entire class in creative ways. Choice is an important factor. Slower students should work with those who are more capable of seeing an activity completed.

Ask students to review the Beatitudes, the spiritual and corporal works of mercy, and state how they could be implemented in their daily lives. Relate them to the TV news reports so they can become realistic and taken out of the abstract where they too frequently remain.

Require that the class read St. Paul on *Love*. Meditate and discuss its application to the needs of these times, to the songs written related to same. Consider the fact that much is written and said, but that there is little consistent action, which demands sacrifice, when it comes to showing love to those who are not immediately within their circle.

Observe or report from a book, a TV program, an incident, a film where people live their faith, where they really light a candle. Observe in relation to being generous in volunteering for a cause, by showing kindness, by being gracious, by being apostolic. Recall the work of Tom Dooley, of Mother Theresa of Calcutta. Make recommendations to your class how they could live their Catholic lives if they were more aware of what was needed and what they could do. Recall no one can go to heaven alone.

If you had the spirit of a missioner, what could you do here at home to make people more aware of their faith? Tell how you would handle each of the following suggestions:

Make your parents and other adults aware of the Religious Education programs available for the laity. Help them to understand the changes in the Church now.

List the different ways you could serve as a teenager, could be a Christian witness such as to help senior citizens, those in convalescent homes, students attending public schools, other incidents and places even if you just brought the spirit of joy and a smile.

Give ways that you could help in your parish, such as in the choir, in teaching religion, in helping the sisters in the grade school, the clubs in the parish, in the community. What could be done to involve other youth who are apparently apathetic, indifferent?

Consider the social issues that confront our present day world. Include the threat of war, destruction by nuclear power which could happen at any moment, the supposed superiority of Russia, the one world government and what it would mean to religion, the increase of Communism which is taking place compared with the want of the increase of Christianity, capital punishment, the need of reform in our prisons, the establishment of more half-way houses, neglected children, and the spread of euthanasia.

Read widely on these topics and others so you will have confirmed knowledge even if it differs, but will not be giving just mere opinions. Give the Christian point of view of what we could do as Catholics. Show the need of leadership and what could be done to bring about change and direct history along a different course.

State what you could do as a young adult to help the hungry throughout the world, the poor in your own neighborhood. How could you use your talents to help the blind? the retarded? the slow learner? How many hours do you give of yourself each week? Remember you might not be able to help people now, but you can prepare through education to help later if you are aware. Think of what they are doing in colleges, the experiments going on to increase the supply of food for undeveloped nations. Find out about the pilot studies that are being conducted. Think of the programs based on love and attention to help slow learners, as exemplified in the olympics that are held annually for these underprivileged children.

Donate two hours each week to baby sitting where a mother who cannot afford to pay could get some rest or a change. Form a club that will offer these services free. Donate time to be a life guard during the summer where underprivileged children learn to swim, teach swimming to youth who are poor, train others to do so, teach a first aid class, plan a retreat for children of different ages that have not had the opportunities to grow spiritually as you have. Realize you have an obligation to help people. They need you.

Think what you could do as a member of a peer group to change the attitudes of teenagers who are selfish, who do not take the teachings of Christ seriously, who do not help people. Make recommendations.

Do you belong to a "Secret Society" when it comes to sharing your faith, talking about Christ or religion? Compare your want of zeal with others who are more apostolic. Have you ever faced up to your own difficulty? Are you failing Christ?

To widen your experiences, and develop leadership abilities, establish small groups among your peers that will plan enriching experiences for others. Include in each group someone who is shy, who does not belong to your clique. Plan and share together these activities you can make possible:

Plan to visit a theater, the art center, the music center, to attend a film, a special program, go to the park with this small group. You can choose something that does not cost.

Visit the science museum, the city of industry, the courts, a cathedral, a mission, a moving picture studio, the harbor, a factory, a market, a shopping center, a bank, courthouse, medical center, employment agency, etc. Observe how things are done, the public relations. Prepare questions so you can act intelligently and learn from this experience.

Share with your class the different organizations in which you are active. They need not be a Catholic group. You could consider at this time the Junior Legion of Mary, the Junior Theresians, Drama groups, Red Cross and comparable organizations that have service as their objective.

Consider what good you could do if you were well prepared and really appreciated your God-given faith: as a teacher, a social worker, a lawyer, a business manager, a senator, an FBI agent, a member of any group who gives service. Be specific. Interview a person involved in any group you report on, considering same from the point of view of service.

Choose one of the following topics and prepare a short talk of 2 to 4 minutes to present to the class. Include the obligations required of each. Select films related to particular topics which can be secured from the local libraries without charge to make the report more vivid. Sometimes a recording could introduce or end a presentation. Several of the reports could be combined, and some could be shared using the panel approach:

Belief in Human Life.
In Search for Christian Power.
Living your Faith as you Prepare for the 21st Century.
Death—What Does It Mean to Me?
Walking with Christ.
Being Counted. Why so few leaders?

People Need People—Develop from Songs.
Youth Hungers for Prayer, for the Spiritual.
Prayer Seminars. What are they? Could you organize one?
Personal Philosophy of Life. What does it do for one?

Consider the needs of the present moment. Cut out pictures that will depict each need, mount. Take a psalm that is related, change title and words where necessary and paste on back of framed picture. Could use a poem or an essay instead. Prepare in relation to the needs of contemporary man such as: Man's Search for Meaning, Death, Destruction, Alienation, Hunger, Loneliness, Growing Old, Unwanted, Handicapped, Neglected Children, etc.

Present personalities to whom students could relate. Have them look up definite particulars about their contribution to help change the world and relieve suffering, such as: Mother Theresa, Damian the Leper, Father Keller, Mother Seton, Mother Cabrini, Tom Dooley, Thomas More, and characters that students would select. Relate to Christ's teachings and different incidents in Scripture upon which they built their lives.

Ask students to list experiences that have helped them in their relationships with others. How did these experiences make them more Christlike?

List experiences that were exciting, were challenging, were motivating, changed your thinking, shocked you, inspired you, brought you closer to Christ, made you a better Catholic. Interview other students or adults to determine their experiences that were enriching personally.

Enriching the Spiritual Life

The traditional teachings of Christ, the once popular religious devotions are not excluded from these religious experience programs. They are part of the Catholic heritage that can be adapted with different emphasis in different ages. Christ is the same today, yesterday, and tomorrow. He belongs to the ages and so does His message which remains important and realistic even amidst change.

To activate students and involve them in the learning process many dynamic techniques have entered the classroom. Large classes are divided into small groups, and provisions are made for personal conferences to vitalize teaching. Students work independently on different assignments and time is assigned for such within the regular classroom. The use of varying techniques and AV materials provide the religious experiences that contribute to the development of their spiritual life. Attitudes are stressed, leadership training is offered, and students are encouraged to develop a sense of responsibility, self-direction, and an intelligent self-concep ˙ ᴇɴriᴄhes their personalities. These religious experiences oft- ᴇ the teacher-child relationship which dominated learning at an earlier period. The teacher creates a climate of mutual respect based on real friendship, not familiarity.

Related Religious Experiences Enter

Closely allied to the formation of youth as intelligent Catholics are religious experiences that will involve them, based upon psychological principles that enable them to learn on their own and to understand themselves as persons with definite responsibilities. Here are a few that could be helpful:

List personal problems that concern them, that discourage them, that make them happy. They need not sign their names. They could be summarized under definite titles. Ask a group to lead a discussion on ways to cope with same, to accept others, and to reject those that will pass away with time. The assignment will reveal much that should enter into the total religion program indirectly. The clarification should help some of their confusion and hurt feelings.

Ask students to bring to class at different times: Ten goals that teen agers have in mind and want to develop. Ten values they want to acquire that would enable them to grow in vital convictions by which they could live. Collect, edit, and duplicate. Have a panel of students consider these in relation to: How realistic they are, how idealistic, how impossible to reach, how sincere they are in listing same, and what they could do personally to live by those which enter into their style of life.

List the qualities that a leader should have; how people are influenced. Give suggestions how they could develop leaders within their class and consider the different types of leaders that are effective.

Have students (seniors) list the qualities of mind and heart they want for their husband of the future, or their wife, and as a father and mother. Show how they begin now to acquire these personality traits that will enable them to be good fathers or mothers.

Encourage youth to talk about themselves. This will enable them to understand themselves and their companions and also will help the teacher direct their activities so they will develop to the fullest as a person.

Consider words using the game *Password*. Note how the students think, react. Have them list different meanings, in relation to their personal life, to religion, and their responsibility to God. Have students choose different words and the related activities such as: happiness, friend, light, peace, love, hope, joy, people, persons, faith, sacrifice, experience, time, life, now, discovery, being compassionate, being important, success, advantages. Connect each word with a quotation from Scripture or a writer.

Ask students to discuss some of the following. Assign and allow a week to prepare. They may read articles that are related, prepare questionnaires to interview people, tabulate their findings, duplicate and share with the entire class:

Christians live in a credit card society.

The philosophy: You are only wrong when caught.

Modern Communication destroys people; influences for wrong.

What do you mean by an Apostolic Teenager?

The destructive problems today are: Drugs, Drinking. How?

What can be done about: slums, poverty, prisons, juvenile delinquency?

Consider the following as problems: Structure, authority, freedom, conscience. Why are youth uptight about these? Are they just following the crowd? Study strategies to involve them so they will not get lost in the false games of life, so they will be able to live in keeping with their potential, and not meet failure.

Developing Christian Values

Secularism with its materialistic concepts undermines society in that it denies God in the action of these times. Advertising motivates the people of our affluent society to acquire the comforts of the world and the pleasures that fail to satisfy. Secularism which dominates the thinking of so many becomes more destructive than communism. Youth are unaware that this creeping philosophy of secularism has become part of their decisions as noted in following the crowd, in keeping in with the "in" group, in accepting permissiveness that leads too frequently to immorality, believing the commandments of God are outmoded, claiming that the Church has changed. Ethical principles no longer exist in high places as noted from the political scandals that contributed to the decline of so many leaders because of their want of honesty and integrity in the Christian values that mattered. To offset the growth of this secularistic philosophy which is so contagious, reaching out activities will enable youth during their formative years to understand and acquire Christian values that are positive and constructive as they become involved in evaluating the consequences of following such, and enter into action that will change these times. Some assignments that the teacher could offer for students to choose are:

Require students to read on secularism and to define it.

Note how it is related to the materialistic concepts by which people make decisions. They should be specific in listing the thinking and actions that are secularistic and are accepted by Catholic teenagers. Have them illustrate how they can be easily deceived. Determine those concepts that are seriously wrong compared with those that are considered as part of the way of life even if not recommended by Christ in His plan revealed in Scripture. Pros and cons will open new ways of evaluating, which might need the direction of the teacher. Draw conclusions that are helpful to the Catholic young adult so he will not be trapped.

Christ in His parables prepared the people of His times to live in keeping with His recommendations. Ask each student to take one parable and to change it into a modern incident related to secularism where possible. Use today's terms and apply the conclusion to contemporary times. With each student taking a different parable and sharing their creative way of developing it, they will come to realize how modern Scripture is.

Require students to read carefully one of the following incidents and to conclude the Christian values that Christ was recommending as He reached out in the religious experiences that were recorded as He met people. Consider the changes that entered their lives. Scripture is the source Christ left man to live in keeping with His plan:

Christ with Mary Magdalen.
The Prodigal Son returns.
The Good Shepherd loves His people.
The multiplication of the loaves and fishes.
An incident of their choice.

Take a popular song or poem and show how the message contains a Christian value in keeping with the recommendations made by Christ. How has it influenced modern youth?

Listen to the record, *The Impossible Dream*. Interpret the

meaning as related to Christian values in relation to:
Death of a student from their class. Death of a mother with
a family from cancer. Death from an overdose of drugs of a
young adult. Death from an accident. Death from suicide.
Death that could have been prevented.

Have students read an essay or poem on death before considering the relationships to life. They have many creative ideas
that would enter into a discussion about the preparation for
death, their own resurrection, judgment, purgatory, hell,
heaven.

Follow this assignment by having students give experiences
they have had with death, with funerals, with consoling families. Ask some to write a letter of sympathy. Draw conclusions.

Consider Christian values by explaining and illustrating the
following:

Ethical living and what you plan to do about same.
Permissiveness before marriage, trial marriages.
Moral values vs. immorality.
Movies that destroy morals.
Interpersonal relationships.
Going steady too long.
Selfishness destroys marriages.
Unwanted pregnancies, unwed mothers.
Divorces are too easy to obtain.
Broken homes cause children to suffer.

Ask students to look up articles on any of the following
which in themselves are intended to form Christian values.
They could be presented after the consideration of the many
factors that are so destructive as suggested in the previous
assignment:

Teen Challenge—a program for drug addicts.
Coffee Houses—a place for young adults to enjoy music
and life.
Charismatic Programs—movement which involves many
Christians.

Ecumenical Programs—have different programs that help better understanding.

Prayer Seminars—a prayerful consideration of the study of Scripture.

Have students realize that they will never develop worthwhile Christian values until they have accepted self, love themselves as children of God, made to His image and likeness. If this concept is understood, students will grow in self-confidence, in developing a well balanced personality, in expressing appreciation, gratitude, in giving love, and accepting love, and enjoying that peace of soul which is so essential to be effective apostles. Consider with students how these qualities of mind and heart can enrich each one's life and ask them to develop a plan that they can implement personally.

Give students meaningful quotes or have them select those that appeal to them. Hold an exchange quotation day having them present the value of each one through a planned sharing experience. Take the phrase, "Lift up your hearts." Relate that phrase to living one's life to the fullest, living with a sense of humor, in the spirit of joy, being happy, spreading happiness, making sacrifices cheerfully without counting the cost of self, being positive, allowing others to live, etc. Draw conclusions by which they could acquire the attitude that enables them to make friends and keep friends. Never take these qualities for granted. Students need to be exposed to ways to acquire such virtues.

Have students explain "being a witness" in light of the monthly *Christopher Notes* which gives so many illustrations, or use the daily meditations entitled *Just a Minute*. A brief consideration of any one of these inspirational thoughts for a period of time would open many challenges to youth.

Conclude this study of Christian values by students submitting a list of things they could do to live as Catholics to make the world more Christian, to change certain dominant evils, as pilgrims in time who should make a contribution as they walk towards eternity. Encourage them to take a few of these and try to put them into practice in their lives and to consider those that they could implement when they have completed school. This should make them more aware of the fact that religion is not confined to that short period on Sunday when they attend Mass and that it must be lived 24 hours a day and such is possible.

Discuss the application of love through definite incidents in considering the following:

Love needs a word of encouragement.

Love needs a thoughtful glance, an understanding expression.

Love comes alive with a chance encounter, a reaching out.

Show that often the following problems exist because of the want of love, or the understanding of Christ and His great love for each person. Illustrations from life will vitalize the meaning of each concept:

Man in conflict with himself, the lonely man.

Discouraged people, frustrated people, alienated people. You are your own worst enemy.

Living without trust, with anxiety, worry.

The mystery in each person, the cross is part of our lives.

Being superficial, wearing a mask to hide insecurity.

Each group of students should determine the procedure they would like to follow as they prepare to understand and share these varying assignments. They could be reported from books read, TV programs watched, interviewing older people or even their peers to determine their thinking on the many concepts suggested, evaluating what their previous study of religion has done for them with comparable experiences. Having spent some time on evaluating their relationship to Christ through the study of Christian values, their spiritual life should have deepened.

Sharing Religion Values with Parents

Students should be encouraged to prepare programs and to present them at parents' monthly meetings, or as a series of adult education programs at a particular time, or for a period once a month in the morning for mothers, or for an afternoon period for a different group. Students are being trained as leaders, as Christian witnesses, to present the Good News, so it should begin in their own immediate circle. Too, many parents are confused, they think that the changes in the church are much different than they really are. There would be a better meeting of the minds if parents participated in these programs which students would present:

Do a religion program based on the principles of the College Bowl programs. Set down the ground rules. Assign students. Appoint a moderator. Keep within certain topics. Give those who are to participate the book or books from which the questions are to be prepared. They can model the programs on any one of the many game shows on TV or adapt them to their needs. Call it by any popular name, such as: *Religion on the Line, Religion is Academic*, etc. Students could select the name and prepare the publicity for same. Many of the new Catechisms could be used, or certain decrees from the Vatican II documents would offer an excellent program. It should be confined to one type such as those relating to religion answers, or to problems in Vatican II.

Conduct a different type program with the same idea in mind to review the basic religion concepts which youth need to know. It could be called *What is My Line? What is My Life? What Answers are Right?* This program will differ in that students from all religion classes are encouraged to write the questions that bother them and place in a box for a period of a month. Religion teachers should encourage these questions. They will need to be edited so that the ones that youth want definite answers to will be included when a panel of students presents them to the entire group.

Present a program on the *Media Influences My Life,* which would also include the press. Students could be selected and assigned certain programs, books, and periodicals to consider their influence in giving them values to live by such as:

TV programs that influence me as a person, as a student, as a Christian. These programs could contribute to the development of character, of personality, as a leader.

Review books, writers, films, periodicals that influence one for good, help them to develop their power of critical thinking, etc.

Hold an *Inspiration Night for Parents.* Prepare and present a program that will include the values that have been studied and that parents would enjoy. The readings could include letters that have become classics, or speeches of great people, poetry readings, and recorded music of popular songs with a message. Also students could prepare their own songs. They could conclude this program with a song fest where their parents would join in the singing. Values should be shared.

Encourage students to plan for another year a different type program that would enable the parents to see what the school is offering in preparing their children to cope with the world. Decide on a list of moral problems that should be considered and choose different ways of presenting the program. It might be a series for each week in Lent which would make an excellent adult educational activity. Here are some ideas.

Present a film on a moral problem or on poverty or hunger. Follow by a well prepared discussion which should involve the parents as well as the students.

Invite a guest speaker to address the group on the *Right to Life* or some other problem. This could be accompanied by a film and discussion.

Hold a panel with faculty members and student leaders based on questions related to attitudes that need to be considered with parents so their thinking will be clarified.

Present a program on drugs, and one on youth drinking. Invite people from these associations that assist people to overcome these problems.

Invite a priest, a doctor, a parent, and a student to hold an open end discussion on a problem not as yet covered.

Organization of Film Programs

Catholic educators do not have to limit films exclusively to those that are religiously orientated. If students were prepared with the directives necessary for viewing films intelligently and if the viewings were followed by discussions on ways to evaluate and apply to life, use could be made of the popular films that have definite messages for the youth of today. They have an artistic touch and are more likely to convey values to the students which is the purpose of presenting the film in the religion class.

The religion teacher should develop within her class a committee who would recommend the films or TV programs that would be related to the intentions of the present doctrines, or to the themes of the class at that particular time. The viewing must have a purpose and the most important part of the lesson is to prepare students to observe, to associate with definite doctrines or values, and to see the relationship to their lives.

For this reason, a definite day does not have to be set aside for film viewing, nor does a period of time have to be devoted to seeing films. In too many cases, this has been busy work, or a means of escape from real learning. There are so many films and TV programs available now that selections can be made that are definitely related to the religion program being followed at that time. This change has to be made if teachers understand the purpose behind the needed attitudes to give students intelligent religious experiences.

The Media Committee of students with the teacher could recommend the films that they think would enrich the doctrines being studied and offer application to their lives in keeping with the teachings of Christ. Here are a few ways they could develop an effective program:

Secure free catalogues from the local libraries. They have excellent films and filmstrips from which to make selections. If the class is following a theme such as on poverty, urban problems, morality, etc., they could choose those short films that would be related.

Follow the *TV Guide* for the programs that might come that week that could be recommended for students to watch. Such assignments are excellent for home work. They need to be prepared so they will know what to observe and then they are more likely to enter into intelligent discussions and applications.

Ask to be on the mailing list of the national TV stations such as NBC, CBS, and ABC. They have publications telling of special programs that they plan to sponsor. All these activities relate religion to life which youth expects.

Film Festivals and Related Programs

The high school students could sponsor a film festival for the students in the nearby elementary schools on Saturdays. Such programs lend themselves to many different approaches such as taking a theme, or several themes and showing short films, or preparing a program with a particular actor for several showings. Along with these could be a drama program, a poetry reading presentation, or the forming of singing groups. This would be an activity in keeping with their apostolic zeal that would keep students busy over the week-ends, or could be shared with students who suffer from different forms of neglect and would enjoy such activities.

This type of involvement would prepare high school students to assume responsibilities for worthwhile activities while training them in the techniques of leadership and discussion procedures as they direct the thinking of these children.

Make Films and Slides

Students have their own moving picture machines that could be used to make pictures of religious activities or other enriching experiences that could be shared by the religion class. They could choose a theme like: The Mass, Vocations, Being Involved, or one of their own liking and select the pictures, the readings that they could tape, and show to the class. The same thing can be done with slides. They enjoy such experiences for they are very creative. These could be presented to one of the CCD classes so that others could benefit from them.

Tapes: Teaching

There are so many tapes being recorded today that are definitely related to some of the newer religion programs that youth truly enjoy. Follow the correct procedures in listening, that is, never to be too long at one time. The discussion will help in understanding the message. At times they could be shared with their parents. Also, encourage students to make their own tapes. This is an excellent way to present a program that they have been assigned to develop. Insist on quality or students will become careless.

These reaching out experiences which involve youth can become part of any unit of study as they will enable students to see how religion is related to many phases of life. Teachers might use these experiences to accompany the study of prayer and Scripture that offer youth activities in which they can participate to make their learning experiences more meaningful.

CHAPTER FOUR

ENRICHING YOUR SPIRITUAL LIFE THROUGH PRAYER EXPERIENCES

To know Christ personally, which is the heart of teaching religion, necessitates prayer experiences that will enrich the spiritual life of youth. Teenagers are often confused in their search for Christ. As they come to experience Christ in their lives, they will enjoy that fulfillment for which they long. In order that these young people will meet Christ, will accept His love, and will give their love, teachers must create a climate of prayer through involvement activities. The religion program must provide those opportunities for encountering Christ so that He will become real and personal to students.

Prayer activities that involve youth must enter every year of high school so that they will be exposed to encounters with Christ. A dynamic prayer program can be developed many ways, allowing for change each year. The following suggestions could be adapted to a four year religion curriculum:

One day a week or a month in each religion class take time to exchange prayer experiences in small groups or on the person-to-person basis which would set the stage for creating a climate of prayer for the lower classmen. The program is built on involvement-experiences so students could re-discover Christ as they share their faith observations and learn the different ways He reaches out to them.

A four or six week seminar would offer an ideal program

to deepen the spiritual life of classes. Ideas are given for them to choose to concentrate on so that their prayer life will bring them closer to Christ.

An elective on prayer for one quarter or for a semester would offer an ideal in-depth study for developing Christlike Catholics. There are many publications today to use in connection with this elective.

With the idea of creating an atmosphere for learning prayer, a definite program could be developed so that the activities would contribute to the spiritual formation of students. Plan the program so that the same assignments are not repeated each year. Students should begin by studying the objectives that will direct them in the study of prayer and the different definitions that will clarify their meaning of prayer.

Objectives in Studying Prayer

Since prayer is an integral part of the lives of Christians, it would be of value to consider with youth the purpose of prayer in the objectives which follow. Through this study, students should come to know and realize the need of prayer in their own lives. Later students are more likely to develop personal goals that would be realistic to them. The entire purpose of teaching religion is to enable youth to assume responsibility for their spiritual development. To make this study of the objectives of prayer realistic, have students illustrate each as they observed them in their lives and in the lives of others. These objectives are allied to the experiences in which they will be involved as they pursue these units at the different class levels on prayer:

To indicate how many praise God, thank God through prayer and how frequently students neglect this type of prayer.

To learn how to make acts of adoration, of love, of sorrow, of humility, of confidence, of trust in God through prayerful meditation throughout the day when one recalls God's presence.

To prepare prayerfully at Mass, not to be so passive at Sunday Mass. To enter into those activities that will enable youth to participate prayerfully in the greatest of all prayers, Holy Mass. Consider what they observe on Sundays in their parishes.

To meet Christ as one reads Scripture, reflects on Christ's words to him, converses with Him, listens to Him, and plans with Him. They need to be trained to enjoy this experience.

To read books and essays on prayer so that they enter into their own prayer life more intelligently and with greater love for God.

To realize that prayer is a celebration that needs preparation which enters into the para-liturgical prayer programs that they will be involved in developing and sharing with others.

To understand the different types of prayer.

To become involved in apostolic activities as requested by Christ in Scripture that they might be Christian witnesses, capable of bringing the Good News to others. To be effective requires prayerful preparation and this must be understood.

To understand how dependent they are upon God and how they must call on Him. Do all things with Him, in Him, and through Him. Realize, "I can do nothing of myself, but I can do all things in Him who strengthens me."

To live with a spirit of joy which is a sign that Christ dwells in them. Such will enable them to live generously and not be easily disturbed when they meet a crisis in life.

Definitions of Prayer

The purpose of this study of prayer is to create a climate that will contribute to the deepening of the spiritual life of students. It would be worthwhile to consider different definitions of prayer as they are closely related to the objectives and for that reason they might be considered in one program. Teachers might choose to consider them separately. Have the definitions create this atmosphere for prayer one year, and the objectives another year. If they are based upon the observations of these experiences in others and as the students exchange their findings, each one should become more meaningful.

Prayer is talking to God, listening to Him, conversing with Him.

Prayer is loving God, praising God, adoring God.

Prayer is offering our work, our time, our thoughts, our efforts to God daily and renewing it from time to time.

Prayer is consecrating our lives to God and renewing this dedication at Holy Mass frequently.

Prayer is thanking God for His gifts.

Prayer is praying for others, asking favors from God for them, interceding for those who have no one to pray for them.

Prayer is dependent upon God for success, to help us along the way.

Prayer is realizing God dwells in us, recalling His presence.

Prayer is seeing God in others, in all the events of life, knowing His providence guides us and cares for us.

Prayer is forgiving others, those who have harmed us and not recalling the injustices that we experienced.

Prayer is loving with the spirit of joy, of gratitude, as we bring Christ to others. Prayer is accepting God's will, especially in the disappointments and frustrations that we meet.

Prayer is surrendering ourselves completely to Him, abandoning our lives to Him especially when disturbed or worried.

This study of the definitions and objectives should set the stage for the spiritual formation of the adolescent. As they enter into these experiences which will enable them to understand prayer with a different outlook from just saying prayers, the number of apathetic, indifferent youth should decrease. They are more likely to become apostolic and generous in living their faith.

Directives for Creating the Climate for Prayer

After completing the discussion of the experiences related to the objectives and definitions of prayer, the teacher could give the students an outline for the semester which would indicate the prayer program for that month or quarter. Directives will offer techniques that will enable them to become involved as they pursue the particular assignment on prayer at that grade level. They will enjoy the varied experiences that will involve them in the form of activities:

Give students guidelines that will enable them to locate materials related to the activities. They should be directed how to do research.

Encourage them to choose activities that they will enjoy so that they will deepen their own spiritual life. Inspirational talks by the teacher and personal encouragement are often needed.

Direct the students to watch the different panel approaches used on TV for reporting news, interviewing people, etc. They could vary their procedures for reporting by adapting them to their presentation of prayer.

Require them to read aloud on their own several times before they present any readings. Show them how to interpret Scripture in reading correctly.

Go over the techniques for learning as related to the topic at hand in prayer, such as to develop the imagination when they meditate and go to the scene when they contemplate Christ, to review and drill as they learn again the traditional prayers, ejaculations, acts of love, and the law of association or seeing relationships as they apply what they learn to modern times.

Ask them to read essays or books on prayer as they are related to the different assignments. Give them a list of books that they could use.

Involve them in those experiences that will enable them to

share what they have learned in their study of prayer with those who have not had these opportunities.

Prayer Programs for Ninth Grade Students

The ability to pray must never be taken for granted. Any program on prayer must be different from the program students were exposed to in grade school. Introduce this consideration of prayer with certain passages from Scripture so students can realize how Christ considered the need for prayer, and how He prayed. Continue this once-a-week exchange of ideas by having students choose certain assignments to study in small groups. These involvements will enable them to reach their spiritual potential.

Evaluate Prayer Life

Youth could be challenged by evaluating their prayer life. This would enable them to assume personal responsibility for their relationship with Christ. Let each member of the class prepare several of the suggested assignments and later exchange their thinking in small groups:

How often do you praise God? Describe the meaning of prayers of praise? Why is it so seldom used in praying or is it?

Do you thank God daily at night prayers for His gifts to you? Could you list now ten reasons why you should be grateful to God? What does gratitude really mean to you in relation to God, in relation to saying thank you to people who help you? What special talents has God given you? What has He protected you from? Consider gratitude in relation to your family.

How do you place yourself in the presence of God? How often? What does the providence of God mean to you? What does conversing with God mean to you? Listening to Him? Can you give some experiences?

How could you make your prayer life more meaningful? More personally enriching? Do you realize it is your responsibility and not your teachers or parents?

What about reading Scripture for two minutes each evening as part of your night prayers?

What are your favorite prayers? What does the Mass mean to you? How do you participate in it? Do you prepare for Mass? for receiving Holy Communion? What about your thanksgiving?

How can you prevent routine from entering into prayer life? Why do some people think of prayer as just asking for something?

Spontaneous Prayer Experiences

Review with the class the different ways to develop spontaneous prayer. Require students to give illustrations of these varying types for one minute. Illustrate first by giving examples of spontaneous prayer. If students have had this experience, let them lead this presentation. The purpose is to start in the ninth grade with something different from grade school. Begin this program and insist frequently that students in silence place themselves in the presence of God before they enter into the assignment for the day. Follow by the sign of the cross, which should be made slowly and thoughtfully as they recall the Holy Trinity that they are addressing. This will prevent the rush and routine that dominates prayer so many times. Then give suggestions for them to choose for praying spontaneously such as:

Quotations from Scripture, especially the Psalms that are brief and have a special meaning for them. Require the students to address this prayer to God the Father and to conclude with calling on God the Son. Include certain prayers of request for the needs of people within this prayer.

Verses taken from a card, a poem, an essay that they could exchange on the person-to-person basis or to open the class. Follow the ideas that are suggested in many of the assignments. Ask for a virtue or a special gift as you address this spontaneous prayer to God.

Ejaculations that lend themselves to spontaneous prayer such as "Lord, have mercy on sinners, on those who are neglected for not being generous, for our sins, our faults, our failures." This is essential so they can enter into this part of the Mass and recall the many reasons they call out for God's mercy. Each student should develop these ideas in his own ways and then exchange so they can benefit from the developed programs of each member of the class.

Tragedies as reported in the morning newspaper, or related to a friend, to a member of their family, or a family at school. Tragedies lend themselves to very meaningful spontaneous prayers that students will say with fervor.

Death among families, students; illnesses, sorrows in any form, problems that they are aware of, petitions for success in a particular event direct youth towards excellent spontaneous prayers.

Intentions that students need, or their friends, or their families lend themselves to prayer. Sometimes they should just stand in silence so they can address these needs to God without having to share them with others for they can be very personal.

Gratitude for favors received, from being protected from harm, for success, for petitions already made.

Sorrow for evils that have taken place by persons, among groups, in countries, etc. Have them include the evils that are so destructive to make them aware such as abortions, euthanasia, murders, unnecessary accidents that could have been prevented, immorality that comes in so many forms. Ask them to conclude by asking God to forgive and give direction to those responsible for the moral fiber of our country.

Prayers of the Faithful could enter the religion classroom. Have the leader introduce with a prayer and then have students call out the different petitions. It can also include prayers of thanksgiving, acts of sorrow, etc. Students enjoy this form of prayer because it involves so many, and makes personal their desires and wants. Conclude the prayer by offering all these petitions to God with confidence that He will hear and answer.

Students will suggest other types of spontaneous prayer. From the training to which they have been exposed, they will learn many ways to pray directly to the Lord. Require that each semester, at least twice, the students lead the class in a spontaneous prayer so that this form will become natural to them as they enter into other ways of praying.

Ejaculatory Prayers

Too frequently these ejaculations or brief prayers are not reviewed. With the emphasis upon personal spontaneous prayer, they have been neglected. Just the same a certain number should be reviewed each year of high school. This will enable students to carry out that command to pray always, for ejaculations make such possible, especially as students are encouraged to recall the presence of God frequently and for different reasons.

When students are faced with an accident, with death, with a crisis, they want to be able to call on God and, to do so, these brief prayers must become habitual to them such as the term "God bless" is becoming so today.

Ask students to select a certain number of ejaculations each week to say frequently. Keep a list to see how many are covered so they will become part of their prayer life.

Encourage them to learn those ejaculations that include the Sacred Heart, the Blessed Mother, St. Joseph and the other saints related to their feasts and to the different liturgical seasons.

Consider ejaculations related to the news, the desires of students and the needs of their friends. Offer up these brief prayers for the alienated, the ill, the suffering, those in convalescent homes, in prison, the dying, the neglected, the holy souls.

Take the Seven Last Words and make them into ejaculations that they could say as they walked along or in a particular need such as: "My God, why have you forsaken me?"

Review those ejaculations said at certain times like "My

God and My All" at the consecration of the Mass, or when entering a church, or passing a church. Connect with something and they are more likely to remember and make habitual.

Have students make a list of their favorite ejaculations and exchange with another student, giving the reasons for their choice.

Ask students during the time these prayers are being reviewed to write so many in their Religion Journal. Appoint a committee to collect these and duplicate so the entire class will have these brief prayers to use at a later time.

Traditional Prayers Reviewed

While students are involved in preparing spontaneous prayer, this will be a good time to review the traditional prayers, stressing that they pray them with attention and that they avoid the routine approach.

Take one traditional prayer a week until mastered. Begin by studying the phrases so the students will understand the real meaning. Start with those found in Scripture such as the Our Father, the Hail Mary. Begin each class with a spontaneous prayer, and conclude with a traditional prayer.

Avoid rattling off prayers. Insist that students recite in chorus so everyone can understand each phrase. To make sure that all students really memorize, assign different leaders to start the prayer and have the class answer.

Have them recite the grace before and after meals. Later they can substitute different forms of spontaneous grace.

Recite the Creed as a Profession of Faith. Be sure they understand what they believe. When completed, hold a ceremony with candles entitled "Our Profession of Faith." Ask them to review it each Sunday at Mass. They could be the leaders and the congregation would follow along.

Go over the Act of Contrition phrase by phrase so that it will become a real act of sorrow for their sins. Encourage them to say it each evening before retiring, and to prepare for confession by reciting it before they enter the confessional and carefully after they have been given their penance. Comment on the need for fervor and suggest short acts of perfect contrition that they could say after a particular failing or while driving such as: My Jesus, Mercy. Lord, have mercy on me for my sins, etc.

Include the Confiteor and the Acts of Faith, Hope, and Love. Try different ways to review these so students will be able to recall them in later life. Recite row by row so all students will enter into the prayer.

Consider other prayers that should be memorized such as the Hail, Holy Queen, the Memorare, an Act of Consecration to Our Lady, Prayer before a Crucifix, Come Holy Spirit, and any other traditional prayer.

Prayers to the saints might be suggested if they are brief, especially those prayers for their canonization.

The Litany of our Lady or to the Sacred Heart should be reviewed in a particular program but they should not be memorized. Students should know them so they could choose to recite them from time to time.

The school should develop a prayer program suggesting a certain traditional prayer be said at the beginning of each period, allowing one period for choice of any form of prayer. Then students will have an opportunity to master all the prayers they should know. Vary these required traditional prayers each semester so all will be covered each year.

Though the programs developed for spontaneous prayer ejaculations and traditional prayers are recommended for the freshman year, they could be incorporated into the sophomore year if not completed earlier. Agree on which ones would be stressed each year so students will be exposed to these ideas and additional ones that the school recommends. Do not spend too much time on any one semester on traditional prayers for these were learned in the early grades. Yet, organize the program so that they will be reviewed and will challenge youth to make them part of their prayer life.

Sophomore Year

The suggested enriching activities on prayer for the sophomore year are different from those included in the freshman year. At times, the recommendations for prayer programs that were not completed might become part of the next year's program. If assigned to small groups, they could be covered in the once-a-week or once-a-month prayer conferences. These prayer programs could be part of a unit of study or an elective as in the sophomore year when students study the life of Christ or the New Testament.

The dialogue activities that introduce these suggestions for teaching prayer could be developed at any time during the year. They are intended to make students aware of the ways they can deepen their spiritual life. Each year a comparable program is included in order to encourage youth to assume personal responsibility for their own prayer life. Evaluation alerts them to the many experiences in which they could choose to become involved.

In the sophomore program, meditation is presented only in preparation for a more detailed study of meditation during the upper years of high school. Like all forms of prayer, meditation is an on-going process. The involvement activities in the review of the Psalms, and the suggested prayer readings offer enriching ideas related to meditation. Preparing examinations of conscience will open other avenues of mental prayer for they will also require acts of love and sorrow with a firm resolution of amendment which will enable these young people to walk with Christ.

Begin early in high school to develop prayer programs in song, in encouraging the formation of small music groups, in listening to the musical classics and the popular songs which include religious lyrics with a message. These music experiences will assist students to create paraliturgical celebrations which are part of the programs recommended. They involve youth in keeping with the liturgical year which creates an ideal climate to pray with the Church as it renews each year Christ's walk on earth.

Note that the entire recommended program is student-oriented. Directives are given that students can follow and must assume responsibility for developing programs that indirectly will enrich their own personal spiritual lives. The teacher gives the guidelines, directs the activities, including the motivating forces that encourage prayer.

Dialogue on Prayer

Since the upper classmen will be involved in long-time assignments on prayer, perhaps some of the following activities that might be considered as dialogues on prayer or discussions that provide a review of prayer could be selected by different students and shared with the class. They should be studied in light of their relationship to the personal enrichment and spiritual development of the students. These could be independent assignments, not required of all members of the class:

Exchange ideas that will illustrate personal, spontaneous prayer, meditation, and formal prayers. Have students review these different forms of prayer so they will become a part of them.

Discuss difference between *saying prayers* and praying. Refer to the Vatican II mandates on prayer to determine this difference. Show how *saying* prayers becomes a security blanket or a routine and one not meaningful. Illustrate with quotations from Scripture about praying, and selections that lend themselves to prayer.

Ask students to illustrate liturgical prayer. Have them give the other students a pattern on how to enter into the Mass and to participate more fully in their offering of self. Consider at the same time some of the para-liturgical programs, especially those that have been used in their religion classes.

Suggest that a small group of students bring illustrations on prayer from late records, poems, songs, Psalms, prayers of the Mass, traditional prayers, prayers composed by saints, ejaculatory prayers. They can present each in any form they want. It could lend itself to a cassette recording to share with other classes.

Relate different prayers to an article in the morning newspaper which too frequently reflects the sorrows and tragedies of people. This would help youth to pray for these people in need when they are unable to help them otherwise. This should lead to an excellent discussion on prayer in the lives of everyone.

Consider the need of prayer in relation to their particular work, the apostolates of the church, the mission in life given to everyone, the need for vocations, that there will be more happy marriages, the success of an assignment, the needs of the students and their families in the class. Develop prayer on quotations from Scripture, especially those that show how we must ask God and depend upon God for His help. Youth must come to know they can do nothing of themselves but that they can accomplish much if they call on God.

Read chapters from books on prayer. Exchange the ideas gleaned from these readings by duplicating some of the quotations and sharing with the entire class. An intelligent discussion should follow.

Consider prayer in the form of praise, thanksgiving. Read the Psalms that reflect these two themes. Write them in other words making them more modern.

Review the Way of the Cross by relating each station to social needs of now. The teacher might have to make some suggestions in order for students to complete on their own. Base it on Scripture.

Discuss God's presence in the world now, in each student, in relation to the Resurrection. Consider some of the articles that explain His Presence. Relate to His Providence in their lives.

Recall the place of the Holy Spirit as revealed in the

Gospels, as given to each student at Confirmation, as stated in the decrees of Vatican II.

Encourage students who so desire to form their own prayer groups as do the members of Congress, business men, youth groups, etc. A few could share Scripture and prayer with students not in their class or in their school.

Discuss devotion to our Lady. Review prayers that they like, also songs in her honor, the Rosary and its mysteries, Scripture references to our Lady and the teachings of Vatican II on Mary, Mother of the Church.

Review the important feasts of our Lord and our Lady so students will really enter into the liturgical year and review the prayers related to same. Give the origin of each. Some are to be found in Scripture and others in tradition, etc.

Encourage students to make slides, prepare materials of explanations, or prayers, or poems, with accompanying lines from songs. Students who know how to take pictures could work on such programs as:

Scenes from nature that would lend themselves to prayers or poems. Prepare cassettes to accompany the slides. Different parts of the Mass could be pictured and slides made. Other students could explain on a cassette. Pictures of our Lady could be taken from Christmas Cards. Relate to her titles and feasts and prayers.

Photographs from magazines might illustrate the Beatitudes, the social virtues, the needs of people. They could be accompanied by Scripture sayings, prayers, or other explanations. Slides could be developed on the prayers of the faithful that are offered at Mass.

Ask students to prepare brief Scripture services to open class on a special feast day. Also assign students to end class each day with a brief meditation or readings that will be one or two minutes.

Hold a sing-a-long once a semester. Have students direct, duplicate words, secure the music, and make it a form of prayer. Students need to memorize words of songs so they will be with them in later life.

Have a group prepare invocations for special events. Present to the class. Duplicate so they will have them when they are called to open a program with an invocation.

Listen to the news on TV on a certain night and have students list all the people and things they need to pray for that night. Exchange these ideas the next day. Encourage students to become aware of the needs of others and to pray for them.

Prepare a banner with a brief idea on prayer. Have students make neat and attractive banners to display. They could be hung in the church or some public place.

Consider the reasons for apathy, indifference, laziness in regard to prayer, people who go to Mass and do not enter into the Mass, people who pray only when they want something and neglect to thank God if they receive an answer. What can be done about this?

Prayer through Meditation for Lower Classmen

Youth today have a deep interest in meditation. It might be due to the spiritual longings within them. They enjoy this experience. At first, work along with the class when presenting some of the ways people meditate. More details with suggested programs will be offered for the upper classmen.

Present a pattern which should be simple and brief which should require just two minutes. Begin by creating the climate to meditate by recalling the presence of God.

Read one minute from Scripture, a Psalm, a verse. Think for one-half minute in silence, or longer. Conclude with a resolution to apply to life.

The two-minute read-think-act meditation is easy to learn and encourages the development of one idea at a time. It lends itself to many applications related to their lives.

Closely allied to the brief method explained is another one

that might be more helpful in forming Christ in the students through meditation:

Recall the presence of God within you. Take time. Read or listen to what is being considered. Think quietly and lovingly about what is being read to you. Talk with Christ about His message as it comes to you. Give Him your affections prayerfully with acts of love. Make a resolution and ask Him to help you keep it. Conclude by thanking Him for coming to you with His gifts.

Another form of meditation (often called the social inquiry method) which is related to the learning process follows the observe-judge-act approach. This is self-explanatory and could be used with Scripture quotations or with an incident.

The act method of meditation is easy for students to follow as they learn to meditate. Teachers should illustrate each one of the fervent acts of devotion as outlined in this scheme for meditating:

adoration, make acts of love;

humility, make acts of unworthiness, dependence on God;

contrition, make acts of sorrow, ask forgiveness;

thanksgiving, make acts of gratitude, of appreciation;

petition, make requests for spiritual and material needs;

confidence, make acts of trust, of hope, of faith.

Always conclude with a resolution, a realistic one that could be kept. Be definite. Make it personal.

The Psalms as Prayers

The Psalms have a great appeal to the youth of today because of the type of music that they enjoy, especially Gospel singing. They are ever ancient, ever new, for they have a particular message for people at different times. There are many references that would help students understand their meanings. Students could be encouraged to select these Psalms to meditate on for different reasons. Some of the activities in which youth could be involved are:

Select a Psalm that has a special meaning for you and read slowly and prayerfully a few verses. Have a "Psalm Sharing" period; have students exchange their favorite Psalms by reading them to the group, giving reasons for their choice.

Take another Psalm and change the words into the language of the day. Be sure you keep the message. Choose background music to accompany it when you dramatically read it to the class or a group.

Make a list of the Psalms that you think would be of value if you were assigned to prepare a Bible Vigil for a wake.

Go over the Psalms and select one that could replace the words to a spiritual folk song that is popular.

Make a list of the Psalms or verses that could be prayers in time of sorrow, when discouraged, in time of any need. This assignment would make an excellent discussion program on God's concern for men and their dependence on Him.

Ask students to take a Psalm and use it for night prayers for a period of time. It could become their evening meditation before retiring.

Select the Psalms of praise and thanksgiving and use them in preparation for the reception of Holy Communion or for thanksgiving after Mass.

Make posters of bright paper with abstract forms, using brief verses from certain Psalms.

Prayer Readings

Prayer readings lend themselves to varied presentations which students enjoy. Through these reading experiences they become acquainted with authors and books whose writings contribute to the deepening of their spiritual life. The activities that youth could participate in would enable them:

To enjoy a quiet reading period at different times in the class room for a short period now and again. Students need direction in making a choice. Through the inspirational reading of certain selections by the teacher, the class would be motivated in making decisions in keeping with their likes and desires.

To present dramatic reading programs to share with the entire class, one a day for a period of time, or to take an entire period and offer a complete program with varied types of readings that should be presented dramatically.

To share from the book selected, with small groups or on the person-to-person basis, some of readings they have enjoyed. It would be good to read these poems or essays to their parents or another not connected with the school.

The more students can be exposed to the beauty within poetry or in readings of any type, the more inspirational will be their lives. There are many tapes that would serve the same purpose and they could prepare their own tapes to listen to later. Encourage them to keep a bibliography on what they enjoyed. They could recommend to someone who has comparable interests. These readings could be used in the CCD class they teach or in a retreat they assist in sponsoring.

Suggested Readings

Many of the books listed under meditative readings could be used with this program. If teachers receive the catalogues from the different publishing companies they will keep alert of the many booklets and paperbacks that are most attractive and available. Some sources are:

Be Not Afraid—Vanier, Jean
Simplicity—Lefebvre, George
Finding God— Louis Savary, S.J. et. al.
Finding Each Other—Louis Savary, S.J. et. al.
Religious Life of the Adolescent—Heyer, Robert

The Learning Community—Penda, John
Holiness—Larsen, Earnest
Open Spirit—Boros, L.
That Man is You—Evely, Louis
Still Point in a Turning World—Link, Mark, S.J.
The Gift of the Sea—Lindburg, Anne
Moments of Meditation—Elroy, Paul S.
Meditations, a Spiritual Journey—Bloom, Archbishop A.
Surprised by the Spirit—Farrell, Edward
Prayer is Hunger—Farrell, Edward
Contemplative Prayer—Merton, Thomas
Thoughts in Solitude—Merton, Thomas
Seeds of Contemplation—Merton, Thomas

Songs are Prayers

Time could be spent in class in learning spiritual, religious, Gospel songs which are so popular. Students should be trained in the hymns that are sung by the entire congregation in their parish churches. Too many can only sing the first line so they do not make singing at Mass a real prayer. There are many ways old songs can be reviewed and new songs taught.

Begin classes daily or each week with a song for a month until they have mastered a group of songs, or take a day now and again and have a song fest for the class. Let them choose the ones they would like to sing.

Use the students who have talents to direct the singing or to help with it in different ways. Appoint a committee to prepare the song sheets, to accompany with guitars or pianos. Others who are capable could direct the group.

Tape songs with the words from the records to help teach the class. Students who can sing could sing the words and tape them to give tonal quality to the singing.

Prepare for class or school Masses carefully so students will appreciate the beauty of the Liturgy. Learn the main parts of the Mass so they can be sung. If possible, learn them in Latin.

Learn also the beautiful songs that were so meaningful that are now returning in Latin.

Group Singers

In addition to student leaders who can help with the direction of the singing in class or in the parish, there are many students prepared to form groups of 2, 3, or 4 to develop programs on their own. They could present them at school, in their parishes, or in the community. Youth of other faiths have so many of these small singing groups which they have developed themselves, and if encouraged, our students would do the same.

Have them select a name for their singing group. They can include other than religious songs in their offerings. This is a good way of spending leisure time on something enjoyable.

Encourage them to help by offering these programs to CCD classes where the teachers could bring beauty in song to their classes.

Suggest that students who play musical instruments form their own small groups so they can offer programs to people when needed. Insist that they practice and that they strive for excellence in any presentation.

Musical Recordings

During quiet time in a religion class plan programs where students can listen to recordings that are popular and others that are classical. Students could bring their own or they could tape some from the radio or TV programs and share them with the class.

Listening is an excellent assignment. Afterwards, if teachers desire, they could evaluate with the students this experience.

The public library has a large selection of these recordings so there will be no difficulty in obtaining same. Also, go to a local bookstore or music store and locate some of these musicals that students would enjoy during this quiet listening period. Or send to the companies and secure their catalogues before ordering:

Religious Music published by the Ave Maria Hour, Graymoor Monastery. Graymoor, New York.

With Joyful Lips, Biblical Hymns and Psalms, World Library of Sacred Music. Cincinnati.

Missa Luba, Mass sung in Congolese style.

Mozart's Requiem, Sung at a Pontifical Requiem for John Kennedy. RCA Victor, New York.

The Messiah, by Handel, Angel Record Company, New York.

Elijah, by Handel, Angel Record Company, New York.

Messiah, by Handel, Sung by the Memorial Tabernacle Choir, Columbia Masterworks.

These are only a few. Many monasteries have recorded choirs chanting the classics of the ages that students could listen to.

Examination of Conscience for Teen Agers:

Work with students in preparing an examination of conscience. Even if they do not use it regularly, to have to prepare one will re-acquaint them with sin and their responsibility towards sorrow and a firm resolution of amendment. With more frequent communal penance services in the parish churches this program should be helpful. Also it should alert youth to the need of God's forgiveness and the graces received through this sacrament.

Build this examination of conscience on the Ten Commandments, the Beatitudes, the Spiritual and Corporal Works of Mercy. They could use the ones found in prayer books to get an idea and select those that are related to their lives. *Youth Before God*, by William Kelley, offers fine thoughts for students of this age to evaluate their relationships with God.

Try to include sins of omission as well as those of commission, neglect as related to justice, obligations that they assume, mandates from Christ as recorded in Scripture, especially those related to their prayer life and the sacraments.

Concentrate on God's love and mercy so students will not

fear confession in later life if they should fall into serious sin. Consider the need for a firm purpose of amendment and the importance of their act of sorrow while the priest forgives their sins in the name of Christ, as His representative.

Encourage them to think how they can grow in certain virtues and their prayer life. Here is a good time to make a resolution for the penance they will perform to replace having to abstain from meat on Friday or fast during Lent. Often they neglect this obligation.

When the students have completed this preparation for confession have the committee edit and duplicate it so all the class will have a copy. Then ask another group to make a very brief examination that they could use each evening that they might learn to advance spiritually. At least they should be aware of the need of saying an act of contrition formally or in their own words before retiring each evening. All these experiences are needed if they are to be formed as Christians who can go on their own in later life.

Junior Year

To change the pace and the form of teaching prayer, one week a month could be devoted to the exchange of ideas and programs developed during this year. Give the assignments one month in advance so students could be working on them to share at a later date. From time to time, some of the activities of the earlier years could be included. To illustrate:

Review of the traditional prayers of the Church as an introduction to the opening of classes. Conclude with short ejaculations so that students will learn them by heart and that they will become part of them.

Pray in silence at the beginning of class so students will continue to recall the Presence of God then, and other times throughout the day.

Short meditations, the reading from Scripture, from poetry,

from verse cards that students would choose to begin class for a month or so. Readings from happenings recorded in the newspaper would give them intentions for which to pray at least once a week before class.

Other activities that are short would lend themselves to daily class prayer. They could be chosen by the student leaders. These different ideas would offer youth an excellent review.

Bible Vigils

Students are now familiar with Scripture, with books on prayer, with readings, poetry, and comparable activities that would enable them to develop meaningful Scriptural Services. They could select different themes or prepare Bible Vigils for special liturgical feasts as the main assignment for this year. Assign a small group of students to direct each activity and to prepare the program in which the entire class will participate. If the Scripture Service is outstanding the program could be presented to other classes or to the entire school. Copies of each should be kept for use in future years, or a book could be compiled for that year for students to use in later life.

Demonstrate the different ways the class could participate in these Scriptural Services. See that the class has copies of books containing Bible Vigils. It would be effective if students did not use the ones already written but adapted the needs to the special feast. Students with creative minds will introduce many changes. Keep Vigils short so students can enter into these programs prayerfully and meditatively.

Scripture Services can be prepared for the following feasts or in keeping with some of the themes included:

For Advent. (Could use also the Advent Wreath prayer program.)

For the Incarnation. (Follow Scripture, use the Christmas Hymns.)

For the Feasts of Epiphany, Corpus Christi, Sacred Heart.

For First Fridays, for First Saturdays.
For Lent, for Holy Week.
For Feast of Christ the King.
For All Souls, All Saints.
For different feasts of the Holy Eucharist.
For Pentecost, the Feast of the Ascension.
For Thanksgiving.
For our men who died in the service of their country.
For the missions, for vocations.
In honor of Mary, her different feasts and titles.
In honor of Christ, the Great High Priest. For Church
Unity Octave.
For peace.

Communal Penance Services

Closely related to Scripture Services are communal penance programs which students could include in this assignment at least four times a year. Since communal penance services are likely to be part of the Catholic life of the future, youth should be prepared to participate in these programs. Many have been written. *Celebrations for Penance*, Reverend Francis Gross, S.J., offers ten examples of programs that follow the liturgical seasons of the year. The teacher needs to find good illustrations of examinations of conscience to incorporate into these programs that would make youth aware of sin and encourage them to have sorrow for their sins and make firm resolutions of amendment.

Prayer Celebrations

There are many ways to celebrate different feasts. Students should be encouraged to work on these liturgical celebrations so that when they establish their own homes, they can become part of the teachings that they will give their children. Some of these lend themselves to the use of candles. Creative minds will carry out these home devotions many ways. Students could make booklets so they will have ideas or patterns to follow later:

Advent: Have students make their own Advent wreath. The leader could duplicate the prayers, light the candle and follow this custom and other related activities each week of Advent.

Christmas: Develop with students the complete story of the Incarnation. Have two choirs, one a verse choir, and the other a singing choir. Begin with Scripture readings from the Annunciation, and go through the different events leading to the Birth of Christ in Bethlehem recited by the verse choir. In between have the students sing songs related to Christmas. This could be presented to the parents or used in a school assembly.

Church Unity Octave: Use the prayers for the feast when we pray that all will be one. Use lighted candles each day and carry out the theme, "Let there be Light." Also prepare students by having them give reports on how this octave was established.

Lent: Determine the different sacrifices that students could make during this beautiful season of preparation: They could light a sacrifice candle each day or each week. Let them draw sacrifices that they will make. Encourage them to donate to the missions that they might bring the good news to others. They also could write meditations on: The Seven Last Words, the Sorrowful Mysteries, the sorrows of our Lady. Use Scripture readings in preparation.

Retreat: Have them prepare a mini-retreat. There is much material available that they would enjoy. This retreat could be held after school, or two days during the religion class in Lent could be devoted to same.

Holy Week: Go through those services in class so students will have a more intelligent understanding. Close with the students renewing their Baptismal vows using candles.

Pentecost: Have students write brief prayers or essays on each fruit and gift of the Holy Spirit. Introduce with the coming of the Holy Spirit at Pentecost as related in Scripture.

Have students make personal resolutions at the end, silently. Light a candle as they read each prayer or essay.

May: Hold a beautiful May procession. Sing and say the Rosary. Walk around the grounds if possible. Stop at the different shrines. End at the chapel. Have students consecrate their lives through our Lady to Christ. Light their candles at the consecration.

June: Work on a meaningful consecration to the Sacred Heart that could be used in their homes. Encourage students to have their homes consecrated to the Sacred Heart. Review the promises of the Sacred Heart given to St. Margaret Mary.

The May or June celebration could be a family affair held in the evening, when the parents and the other children would join the high school students. Certain classes could assume leadership for the different parts of this procession and consecration of the families.

Meditation

Meditation or mental prayer is popular today, especially among youth. Yet it needs to be taught. Students should be exposed to the different approaches of reflection and then let the Holy Spirit take over as He guides and directs their lives. Teachers should work with students at each grade level until they are able to go on their own. They will choose the method that they will enjoy or find helpful. Since teenagers are easily bored, several techniques in reaching this union with God should be explored. They, in time, will select the way that enables them to listen to the Christ speaking to them in meditation. They long for this intimate relationship with Christ personally and it will come as they deepen their life of prayer, especially through the reading of Scripture.

Listening to Christ in His Word

Select a quotation or reading from Scripture and listen to

His word. Become aware of His presence within you, realizing His love and concern for you personally. You are becoming conformed to the mind of Christ.

Continue to read, to listen. God will reveal Himself to you as you experience His creative, providential, forgiving, and healing love. Renew your consecration to Him with acts of love, faith, trust as you apply the message of His Word to your life now. Do not read too long a time. Stop when His Word speaks directly to you and listen to Christ who awaits your love.

Some of the following Scripture readings will offer students a definite program until they can go on their own. If these were worked out with the class, most of the students would soon be capable of choosing the Word that they think has a special message for them:

For a life of love: (Read John 13:1) "Jesus loved them to the end."

For a life of sharing: (Read Luke 10:16) "He who hears you, hears me."

For a life of union: (Read Luke 8:10) "To you is given the life of mystery. . ."

For a life of friendship (Read John 15:15) "I have called you friends."

For personal identity: (Read John 15:4) "Abide in me, and I in you."

For a life of success: (Read Cor. 15:56) "Thanks be to God for victory. . ."

For a life of prayer: (Read Luke 22:39) "Pray that you may not be put to the test.

Other selections could be taken from the New Testament and given to the students to meditate on for a short period of time, like a week. By that time, they should be able to choose those selections related to the liturgical year, to the Mass of the day, or follow a particular theme that they would like to develop.

The Psalms also lend themselves to beautiful and personal meditations. They express the same hunger and longings that have come down through the ages. Some of the following suggestions would enable students to meditate on their present needs as they reflect on the words as God speaks to them:

Psalm 95: Offer God prayers of praise.

Psalm 8: Realize the greatness of God and the dignity of man.

Psalm 84: Recall God's presence for He is everywhere.

Psalm 145: Reflect on God's great personal love for me.

Psalm 147: Realize God's providence guides and directs us.

Psalm 149: Continue to praise God everywhere and always.

Psalm 50: Be sincere in your praise. God does not want hypocrites.

Psalm 82: God cries out against social injustice.

Psalm 100: Give thanks to God always and everywhere.

The Psalms offer youth delightful prayers to praise, thank, and love God as well as to ask from Him certain favors. Many of the Psalms offer youth ideal prayers for each evening before retiring, in preparation for Holy Communion, and as thanksgiving after Holy Communion. Having learned to meditate students will express these Psalms in their own words and develop different forms of spontaneous prayer that have depth and meaning.

In addition to students reading directly from Scripture, students could be given a few brief quotations for them to think about for two or three minutes and then share their reflections with the entire class. This method might help others who are not so quick in developing techniques of meditation. Here are a few:

"Sing to the Lord with thanksgiving."

"Where are the other ten?"

"Give thanks to Him for He is good."

"Nor do I condemn you."

"I came that they might have life."

"As the Father loves me, I love you."

"Perfect love casts out fear."
"Perfect love is union with God."
"God so loved the world that He gave His only son."
"You will receive all that you pray for provided you have faith."
"Unless you change, and become as little children."

Students will have their own brief quotations and should be encouraged to bring them to class. Give them time to meditate on one each day for a week or so. Then have them share their thoughts with one other student. If they exchange their reflections with different students each day for a short while, they will observe how they can grow in listening to God who speaks to them in different ways through His word.

Making Acts, a Form of Meditation

Another approach that teachers could involve students in as they try to teach them different forms of prayer, especially meditation, will enable them to speak to God with sincere acts of love and humility. After they have recalled Christ's presence within them, they could make fervent acts of:

Love: Adore and worship God who is present there and loves you.

Humility: Realize your unworthiness and dependence upon God who has such a great love for you.

Sorrow: Tell Him of your sorrow for offending Him and ask His forgiveness.

Gratitude: Fill your soul with thanksgiving to God for His many gifts to you.

Petition: Ask God for the favors you need from Him, be they spiritual or material. Pray for others, especially those of whom you are indebted, those who depend upon your prayers, and for those who are in need of prayer like the lonely, the alienated, the hungry, the poor, those in prison, in hospitals, etc.

Reconciliation: Remind God to forgive you and to give you the grace to forgive everyone who has ever done you any harm. Recall the many times Christ reminds one to forgive and to become reconciled; never to hold a grudge; to realize that those who do you severe harm are often ill of mind and heart.

Confidence: Make acts of trust in God's providence, His concern for you, His love for you personally so that you will banish all fear and depend upon Him completely.

These acts of love and humility must be real. They might have to enter the field of action and this should be pointed out to students so that they will be open in their prayers. Since each act is a complete study in itself they should be developed one at a time, asking the students to supplement them with illustrations. They should then develop their own prayers including all these acts. Keep them simple. Require them to memorize the different phases of these acts of love so they will remain with them long after the class ends. Review this technique now and again.

Closely allied to meditation is that of making a resolution. If youth could come to understand this need, they are more likely to acquire those virtues that make a true Christian, remove the obstacles that prevent them from growing in union with Christ, and develop Christian maturity. These are the desires of every teacher, who is dedicated to the formation of students to live the Christ-life, and to be apostolic as they advance in wisdom and age in these times. Here is a pattern that could be developed. Work with the students. Do not just give it as an assignment. They need examples so they will have an understanding of what prayer should do in their lives and how they could develop an attractive Christian personality in keeping with Christ's mandates.

Make a definite and practical resolution related to the reflections where Christ spoke directly. See that it is personal and in keeping with the activities of your present life. Be sure to make a plan to keep it. Review it frequently. Realize it will demand sacrifice. Ask God's help for you can do nothing by yourself.

After students have been taught the different ways to meditate especially on Scripture, they should be exposed to other readings that would be helpful in making meditation very meaningful to them.

Senior Year

Follow the same time schedule as that of the junior year, or develop a program that would require one month each semester. Students should be assigned their particular programs to work on early in the year so they will be prepared to present them when the month comes to exchange ideas that will contribute to their spiritual development.

There are many books that could be used in order for these young people to select ideas that they could adapt to present a program that they would enjoy working on during this year. They could work as individuals, as small groups, or as an entire class as each program is developed with the necessary details.

Prepare a bibliography of books on prayer for students to read, one a month or one a quarter. Follow with small group discussions so that they will come to realize the importance of prayer in their daily lives.

Involvement Activities

Select a Mass with a definite theme. Prepare the Scriptural readings, the songs, the prayers of the faithful, the prayers during the period of thanksgiving. See the New Sacramentary for ideas. Duplicate for class use.

Be sure to include a Mass for Vocations, a Mass for Thanksgiving, and one for the intention voted on by the class.

Choose one of the Scripture Services developed in the junior year in preparation for this monthly Mass; also one of the communal services to help students prepare for the receiving of the sacrament of Penance, or in preparation for some particular feast.

See that they prepare a Vigil for the student or member of a family who dies. Select their hymns and Scripture readings.

Have students prepare prayers for a Prayer Breakfast. Could be developed many different ways using Scripture and other readings. Hold a breakfast for the student council and have them each present their Scripture program.

Prepare a prayer program for senior citizens. Have a group visit a convalescent home around a particular holiday and present their program to the patients.

Determine the prayers that should be taught in grade CCD classes and work out a program at each class level or just for the lower grades. Have students determine how they would teach these prayers and how they would involve students in praying.

Review songs so students will really know the words and will be able to enter into the ministry of singing as they participate in the Mass and the different Scriptural Services.

Make banners related to prayer. Do not allow them to submit banners that are not well made. Or they could develop posters; also keep a bulletin board in each religion classroom related to prayer.

Discussion Groups

For the final assignment of the senior year or throughout the year there should be held small discussion groups to evaluate prayer and its relationship to their spiritual development. Each group could choose to study in depth any of the following themes. Through panels, they could exchange their conclusions with the entire class:

Charismatic prayer, what it is, how it is growing, what is youth's relationship to same. Value and purpose would be included.

Contemplative prayer. Study by reporting on different writings and determining why it is so popular. Make a survey to determine what Catholic youth are doing in this regard.

Participation in the prayers of the Mass. What could be done to make them more meaningful? How could they develop a Christian community in their parishes, in school?

Singing at Mass. What is the problem? Why has it failed? What about music?

Consider prayer in their own lives: traditional, spontaneous, Scriptural meditations, realizing the presence of God, living in union with God, seeing God in other people, bringing Christ to others. Come up with definite conclusions and responsibilities they should assume.

Discuss and illustrate prayers of praise, of adoration, of love, of sorrow, of petition, of thanksgiving; silent prayer; prayers of faith, of hope, of confidence in God, of trust; our Lady and prayer, the Holy Spirit and prayer, Christ and prayer, praying to the Father, communal prayer, private prayer, power of prayer.

Consider the neglect of prayer, routine prayer, saying prayers, being apathetic towards prayer, being indifferent, not depending upon God, the need for prayer, praying for others. What can be done?

Have students bring pictures from different magazines; mount them attractively. Give each a title related to a theme. Make up a prayer to illustrate the picture.

Go over the need of prayer for vocations, for priests, for our young people, for sinners, for the dying, for the suffering souls in purgatory, for those who were killed that day.

What kind of a prayer life would you develop in your family when you have one? What prayers would you teach your children by which they would remember you as father or mother? What about reading Scripture in that home of the future? How would you prepare your children for the sacraments, for Sunday Mass?

With this four year program where students have been involved in different prayer activities, they should be prepared to enter the world and continue on their own those devotions that would contribute to their spiritual formation. They have become aware of the need of prayer, ways to pray and the power of prayer. Such should sustain them and enable them to grow in Christ as He leads and directs them. Through this exposition, their hearts and minds have been nourished. In that the program was built upon student direction, and not teacher demanding, and they were free to choose the varying activities, they are more likely to go on their own as the years open up new vistas for them to follow in the deepening of their spiritual life through prayer.

Para-Liturgical Celebrations

The para-liturgical celebrations that were developed in detail during the junior year should be continued in the senior year. They could be considered following different themes. Keep them brief for students tire. Those found in the many booklets published are entirely too long. Students could use them as models, but adapt them to a definite theme for a particular reason. Here are a few references:

Communal Penance Para-Liturgies

Together in Peace by Reverend Joseph Champlin offers beautiful programs that are different and which include excellent examinations of conscience. Each step offers inspirational thoughts that could become part of the many programs that have been suggested. The prayers lend themselves to creative ideas that could be adapted to the preparation for the sacrament of Penance:
A Call to Prayer.
A Call to Holiness. God's Word Asks Forgiveness.
Prayer for Light and Encouragement.
Love for Others. Especially our enemies.

Come, Be Reconciled by Harold Hall, et. al. These mod programs offer youth experiences that they can relate to and enjoy. They consider responsibilities that teenagers too frequently neglect. To illustrate:

Theme: *Kill Me Softly*. Covers psychological, physical and moral killings and their relationships which demand involvement in activities to really understand.

Theme: *Lord, Give Me a Heart of Flesh*, which is a preparation for the sacrament of Penance in Lent which requires reading from Scripture and singing.

Theme: *The Light of Life*. Is based on change and ways to choose life. Offers an excellent program in that it covers many aspects of living.

The entire communal celebrations relate to the psychological needs of youth in keeping with living that wholesome self-concept which directs them towards self-confidence in meeting their responsibilities. There are many other communal penance programs that will lend themselves to para-liturgical celebrations.

For Thanksgiving

Students need to be aware of expressing gratitude to God. This virtue has to be taught and stressed. It cannot be taken for granted. In preparation for the thanksgiving holidays would be a good time to review reasons for gratitude. Here are a few titles that could be changed and presented by the entire class:

Give Thanks to God Who has chosen us to be His People.
Give Thanks to God for His Promises to Us of a Heavenly Paradise.

Scripture Services on Our Lady

An effective way to return to devotions to the Blessed Virgin Mary is to involve youth to prepare Scripture Services in honor of the different feasts of our Lady. *Glory to Our Lord* offers several celebrations for May and October and for particular feasts.

Songs to Mary, and prayers addressed to her could be included. These Scripture Services offer excellent reviews for Scripture readings, basic doctrines, and prayers in an indirect and meaningful way which students will enjoy.

Prayer Breakfasts

Prayer breakfasts are held weekly in many different places and are well attended by men who first meet for prayer and then have breakfast together, or prayer becomes part of the breakfast program. Anywhere from twenty to over one thousand meet for these breakfasts which are sponsored by different companies, organizations, government, and professional groups. With the increase of prayer centers prayer luncheons are also popular, where Scripture is read, songs sung, and testimonies given.

As Catholic educators we should direct our students to plan programs with a purpose. The student council could sponsor a breakfast at the school for the faculty, or to honor the graduates that year, or to express gratitude to a group of teachers for their assistance. Many of the ideas that have entered into their study of prayer would enable students to develop such a program. In order to give them experiences, some of the following might be helpful:

Introduce each prayer breakfast with a Scripture reading in keeping with the theme. Have students select readings that lend themselves as an invocation and type on cards for future reference.

Address the prayers to God the Father. Bring in God the Son. Include a quotation from a historical or noted character that could accompany the purpose of the prayer program.

List the blessings being considered, the gifts given, or any other intentions for this prayer meeting. The many blessings listed and developed in the present Missals would offer students excellent ideas to incorporate into one of these prayer programs.

Prepare a Marriage Ceremony

For senior classes in Catholic high schools, an activity that could be assigned to students would be to prepare a marriage ceremony. Perhaps a committee would choose to do the research related to this program and they would then compile a book for each member of the religion class. This could be a model when they prepare their own marriage ceremonies in the years ahead. They could begin by selecting the prayers and songs for the blessing of their engagement ring if they so choose. Then, plan the wedding Mass by selecting the prayers from the *Missal* that could be used throughout the entire ceremony. Also, they should prepare the prayers of the faithful that would include asking God's blessings on their parents and families. The songs that they would like sung could be listed as well as the details related to the plans they make with the priest before the ceremony. Students at this time should be encouraged to pray daily for a happy marriage as it is in prayer they will reach the heights of their spiritual life.

Christian Vigil, or Wake

Today people have a choice when they mourn the death of a loved one. The evening before the Mass, they may choose to have the Rosary recited, the readings from Scripture, or a combination of these. There are many models available and the parishes have samples of booklets that could be used. Ask students to prepare a model for each of the three programs.

Program One: Select the readings from Scripture, the songs to be sung, and several of the different types of prayers offered. Sometimes that includes a litany related to the person, his family, and to death and resurrection.

Program Two: Select the mysteries of the Rosary, make the meditations, and include brief Scripture readings between the decades. Also include the songs.

Program Three: Decide on how many decades of the Rosary will be recited. Include Psalms, and other readings from

Scripture. There are many that lend themselves to praying for the departed.

They could also choose what they would like to have printed on the memorial card, and prepare the prayers and readings for the Mass the same way. This would be an excellent preparation for death and some consideration should be given to the Resurrection at this time. If students prepared such a program on the death of a classmate, or a parent of one, the entire experience would be more meaningful.

Prayer and Personal Development

Prayer in itself should contribute to the development of the person. Unless one takes on Christ's attitudes and ways of living, of what value is prayer? To attract others to Christ one must acquire that personality that influences, so such people should grow in:

Joy, the saving grace of humor.

Cheerfulness of expression even amidst difficulties.

Calmness in moment of crisis or disturbances of any form.

Graciousness in their consideration of others.

Confidence in one's ability to do all things in Christ.

Decisiveness, yet flexible to change if necessary.

Openness to accept change which comes in many ways.

Generosity . . . willing to share, to give of time and effort.

Serenity and poise as they think for themselves.

Security within as they depend upon God completely for success.

Positive and constructive attitudes in meeting problems.

Understand and know, that frustrations, disappointments, humiliations and misjudgments enter into every one's life.

Acceptance of God's will . . . knowing that the cross will come in many forms and that it is the purifying force that enters every life as it did that of Christ.

During the study of the different phases of prayer, these attitudes and reactions related to living the Christ way could be considered with the students. As they become aware of these, they will be able to share others that are essential so that they will be able to accept God's plan for them in their walk through life.

CHAPTER FIVE

ENCOUNTERING CHRIST IN SCRIPTURE

Teenagers long for God, for that encounter with Christ. They come close to Christ through the reading of Scripture, listening to His Word, and talking to Him as He reveals Himself. Several religious movements have attracted large numbers of youth to Christ during the last decade. Over 50,000 young adults attended the Expo of the 70's, the convention for Christ in Dallas, and at a great sacrifice. Thousands of these same people enrolled in the leadership training follow-up conferences in their own regions later. As committed Christians they prepared themselves through the study of Scripture and prayer to evangelize the world and bring souls to Christ.

Comparable programs continue to emerge with different titles, varying in their approach, as religious leaders plan activities for youth in search for Christ. The media and press have popularized these encounters which involve youth such as the Jesus Movement, Teen Challenge, Youth for Christ, Campus Crusades, Life, or Charismatic Movements which are attracting so many.

Catholic educators, aware of the value of Scripture to the students they are trying to form in Christ have added Scripture classes to the religion curriculum. They realize the need to create a climate for the reading of Scripture so strongly recommended in the directives entitled *To Teach as Jesus Did*. To proclaim the Gospel message of Christ's teachings demands well planned programs which will involve youth in meaningful activities. They come to know Christ personally while the Holy Spirit directs them in their involvement assignments related to the reading and reflecting on Scripture.

Objectives for Scripture Programs

Students know the value of objectives and they are better prepared to enter into the assignments when they realize where they are going, what is expected of them as they choose to work on different activities. These objectives need to be reviewed now and again.

To make the class Christ-centered so students will come to know Him personally as He speaks directly to them in the study of the New Testament and offers a plan to live by in keeping with His teachings. Consider ways.

To enable students to realize their responsibility as baptized Christians to live the Christ life as opposed to the apathy and indifference which so often prevails. Implement by illustrations.

To motivate students to live with faith and hope, to grow in same as they face the reality of the times in which they live with its human conditions, its weaknesses, as they walk in our pluralistic society. Ask them to give incidents that are related.

To learn to live with dignity and a deep appreciation of life as they cope with the secularistic philosophy which is so destructive. Explain the want of respect for life from birth to death.

To apply the basic doctrines given by Christ to daily living as they nurture their faith and apply to daily living eternal truths revealed in Scripture. Review the Creed.

To involve students in those spiritual formation programs that will enable them to participate personally in the graces Christ offers them in many different ways. Have them give suggestions.

To provide readings and directives that will develop the

personality of the adolescent, as he claims he is in search for identity and for complete fulfillment. Both of which are to be found in knowing Christ as a person with His great love for each one of them. Develop with students.

To consider immorality that is so destructive and the ways it could be prevented among their peers if they understood Christ's teachings. Too many are wrecked because they just follow the crowd. List from the morning newspaper, from TV shows the immorality which is accepted.

To have a deep appreciation of the dignity of the person, to respect him and his rights that greater justice will accompany the future. Abortion, euthanasia, the senior citizen, the disadvantaged peoples enter into this.

To prepare youth for the youth ministries, so that they will live as Christian witnesses as they become involved in those activities that will enable them to bring the word of God to others. Have several give a report on different ministries.

To offer leadership training within the religion class so students will be prepared to be active in these newer programs which are built upon living Christ's teachings as revealed in the New Testament.

In order that students will be aware of the changes in teaching religion, and become involved in the many experiences that are suggested, they should be exposed to activities that would enable them to implement each one by giving illustrations on what can be done. At first, just make a brief survey, for each objective should become part of the varying activities as the class progresses.

Involve Youth in Reflecting on Scripture

Religion courses must vary, must offer choices. All students need not complete the same assignment. There must be a quiet time for reading and reflecting on Scripture which is the very heart of the religion curriculum. These assignments must provide

built-in motivating forces. Dynamic challenges that involve youth
will develop that independent and personal life style which enables them to live as Christian witnesses in keeping with their own
personality as they carry out their apostolic mission.

Teachers direct and offer the needed inspiration which enables
students to work independently on their own. Definite and frequent evaluation, for which they are responsible, assists youth in
using their time to advantage as they select the materials that are
related to the particular study in the varying assignments.

Assignments involve students in their search for a more personal relationship with Christ. Several of the Scripture programs
could be combined with the prayer programs for it is difficult to
separate the study of Scripture from the study of prayer.

Religion assignments should contribute to the formation of
positive dynamic personalities so they will come to know and
follow Christ. Serious consideration must be given to the activities which will involve youth. Plan for the exchange of these ideas
within small groups for it is in sharing these findings that real
learning takes place which leads to realistic action.

Directives for Developing Religious Experiences

Divide the class into five groups with each one taking a
different Gospel and the Letters of St. Paul. Have them locate
the promises Christ made. Exchange these findings with the
group; summarize and duplicate for the entire class. Ask students to live by those they choose for the entire month and
to be accountable to themselves. They need to make a plan
that they could follow.

Have the group continue working together and using the
same readings for other assignments. They could select people
that were described in the Gospels and the places where they
met them. Cut out pictures from periodicals that would relate
to the incident. Give it a title. Complete it with selective Scripture quotations that will illustrate same. Mount neatly and
display around the room.

Make a list of ways that Christ would have answered the following problems: backbiting, telling lies, undermining, double crossing, being hypocritical, phoney, being negative, pessimistic, not trusting people, griping, complaining, spreading rumors, blaming others, not facing facts. Confirm your explanations by relating to Scripture readings. They could be studied in the light of developing the virtues that were recommended, with the idea of leading a Christ-like life.

Spend some time considering why so many do not live as Catholics in keeping with the Scripture recommendations. Is it because they do not read Scripture, or that Scripture has no meaning for them? Could it be that they have not come to know Christ personally? Relate these failures of living the Christian life to the large number of unhappy homes, uncared for children, divorced parents, the immature reactions that prevent people from living to the fullest; killings, suicides. Take incidents from the daily papers to illustrate. Students will come up with happenings in their own families. Determine why so many who are called Catholics are Catholic in name only. They could recommend a program that might contact some of these people, especially through small Scripture groups where people really get to know their responsibility to God. This is the work of the laity and the students of today will assume responsibility in future years to help weak or fallen-away Catholics return to Christ.

Have other groups determine how Catholics could live as Christian witnesses, especially the many fallen-away Catholics, or those who go to Mass only on Christmas and Easter. Have them make recommendations related to Scripture that might help these people. If each student contacted one such person, consider the change that would take place.

Ask students to interview others to determine if they read Scripture and to encourage them to do so. Question their parents, college students, other students. Draw up a program that would be positive in approach to involve those close to them to read Scripture, how to recommend such, what reading

Christ's Word means to them, what changes have taken place. Develop testimonies as those of other faiths do. This is an effective way.

Consider people in the light of the Gifts and Fruits of the Holy Spirit. Observe for one week people met by students, seen on TV, in a film, read about in a book and note if they were accepted or rejected, wanted or not wanted, loved, gave love; lived with peace and joy, were generous, gracious, thoughtful. Ask students to compare those they have observed from the positive point of view with other incidents and have them give suggestions how some of these virtues could be acquired. This should help them in developing their own personalities.

Review the institution of the Blessed Sacrament as stated in Scripture. Meditate on what happened. Read explanations of the institution of the Holy Eucharist, the first Mass at the Last Supper, the great High Priest and His farewell to man. Have them prepare questions (to ask different types of people such as adults, their parents, college students, peers). Why do not people make visits to the Blessed Sacrament if they believe in the Real Presence? Why do not more go to daily Mass? Why do not people really prepare for Mass, why do they not participate in Mass on Sunday? What is the reaction of students to the Mass? This is a very important survey. It could be taped. Recommendations should follow.

Have students select brief Scripture quotations and make spontaneous prayers from each one, concluding with a different ejaculatory prayer so that these brief prayers can be reviewed. Have them memorize at least ten Scripture quotations, so they will become part of their lives.

Ask students to give Scriptural quotations which reveal different doctrines that Catholics believe. Share these Scripture findings with four other students and have each add to their lists. Then ask the students to choose one of the following titles and write: My Creed Expressed in Prayer, or Prayer is,

Faith is, Hope is, Love is, Happiness is. Include Scripture quotations in part of the essay.

Plan your own inservice program for growth in praying with Scripture. After being exposed to the different ways to make it vital in your own personal life, select one of the spiritual books that you enjoy and read for ten or fifteen minutes each day. Note how related many of these books are to Scripture.

Experiences in Encountering Christ in Scripture

These experiences which are related to encountering Christ in Scripture lend themselves to one year's study, to one semester, or as an elective for a period of time, or they might accompany a particular unit of study. They are so developed that students could work on their own, using the laboratory approach, with different ones choosing certain assignments and sharing their findings. All students do not have to complete the same activities. They might be considered as mini-seminars, where through the exchange of ideas, the entire class will be exposed to those experiences that will enable all students to apply Christ's teachings to their own lives. Encourage youth to make personal resolutions as given within the directives so they might live as Catholics and grow closer to Christ.

Teachers could choose those assignments that are related to the student's age, background, and the present study of religion. Never give in to that pressure that all these experiences must be completed. Learning ceases and growth is not possible. They might be studied at another time, when students have completed other phases of religion. Then, they are more likely to understand what Christ is asking of them.

The flexibility even within certain themes chosen for the study of Scripture should create a climate for learning. Within this atmosphere, youth are growing in the knowledge of Christ, His plan for them, and an appreciation of their responsibility to bring the Good News to others. These activities should be inspirational and highly motivating, otherwise they become self-defeating and just another assignment to complete.

Students should work individually, or with partners, or in small groups. The teacher must prepare them for this approach and should work with them until they are able to go on their own. Do not follow the order of any of the suggested programs in studying Scripture. Adapt each to the abilities and interests of students. The directives that follow will give ideas on how they can make religion, and especially Scripture, meaningful. Some activities could be chosen each year as part of a unit so youth will continue to develop their religious life.

It is hoped that after students leave high school they will have come to appreciate Scripture and the place it plays in their own lives. For that reason, recommendations are given in the last group of suggested experiences so that youth can continue, as part of their daily prayers or meditation, the reading of Scripture at different times in ther lives.

Each assignment would last for several days, or for a week. Students should work quietly in the room where the materials needed are available. Using this laboratory approach, these young adults could learn the techniques of independent study. Later they will report back to the group doing the research. Quiet or soft music would add to the atmosphere. Teachers would become consultants or directors of the activities. They would assist the members of the class to locate additional materials. Each group would choose any one of the following to complete:

Characters met as He walked along the way, and places He visited and what happened at these visits. Report for TV news. Use any technique.

Christ in prayer, the time He taught His disciples to pray, the places He prayed, the prayers said, how He addresses His Father. This lends itself to a beautiful and inspirational presentation. Dramatic readings would add to the meaning of Christ's recommendation to pray.

The parables. Re-write in modern terms, using modern incidents, and make application to here and now. This assignment would take an entire week and should be divided among all members of the class, allowing each to choose his own parable.

Christ performs miracles. Review each one. Go back to the place where the miracle took place and give an exact account of the people. Make the needed applications. Consider the miracles that are attributed to Christ in these days.

Follow Christ in His Passion. Comment on the people whom He meets and what part they played in the lesson they have for each one of us now. Follow Him to Calvary where He gives His farewell to us from the pulpit of the cross. Take each Last Word and make applications to people who live in these times.

Christ meets friends along the way. Some know Him, and others do not until He has left them. Describe these encounters with people and have students share the message of then and how it is still needed in our time.

Christ gave us a pattern to follow. Think over the mandates Christ gave in Scripture, the recommendations He made for us to live by. Make a list and show how they would enrich our lives if we really carried them out.

Read St. Paul's epistle to the Corinthians, chapter 13, and change into your own words. Apply it to life using some of the late songs to illustrate. Then take the Commandments of God and re-think positively and constructively. Introduce each one with the word *Love* and prepare an examination of conscience for teenagers: For example:

Love your neighbor as yourself. Consider all the ways you could really love those who cross your path and how at times you neglect to do so.

Love your parents and honor them. Consider your attitudes towards your parents. How are parents neglected when they become senior citizens?

Love people and do not try to destroy them by rumors, taking their good name away, and all the other sins you could list.

Continue following these illustrations and complete the Ten Commandments which are too frequently eliminated. Apply the Beatitudes and the spiritual and corporal works of mercy to the Christian life. Consider ways to live each, and also how they are neglected, yet they were given as a plan of life for Christians as stated in Scripture.

Reflect on these readings for concern, compassion, mercy, generosity, in the light of eternity where you will be judged on love, on what you have given away, and that you can not take anything with you at death, noting that all that is given to you in any form was given to you by God to be shared with others, and the more you give the more you will receive. There are many ways these Scripture readings could be vitalized so they would become part of youth's life.

Allow a quiet period during the religion class and have students read reflectively for 15 minutes or less. Give them directives which might include such questions as: How did Christ describe Himself? His mission? His relationship to His Father?

Different students could concentrate on those character traits that would give them an image of Christ. Write some of the verses and quotations in their Religion Journal for further discussion. They could include other qualities of mind and heart of Christ. Write a brief meditation on some thought at the close of this assignment.

Read the Gospel of St. John reflectively. Each day give students a different assignment to start in class and complete at home such as:

Write a brief account of Christ's farewell at the Last Supper.

Give the report on the First Mass, the Institution of the Blessed Sacrament as revealed in John.

Enriching Prayer Life through Scripture

Encourage students, after you have given them some illustrations, to select their own readings related to prayer and to read slowly, reflecting and meditating while applying to their life.

Select a certain time to read and reflect on those selections in Scripture related to prayer each day if possible, at least frequently and as part of your night prayers. After reading, address God the Father through the Holy Spirit and close calling on God the Son as you make this prayer your own.

Take 10 or 15 minutes at first and follow any series of readings that appeal to you as God speaks to your heart. Vary from time to time so these prayers will never become routine. Let the Holy Spirit direct you. Recall God's presence within you.

Dialogue with God. Begin by recalling His great love for you and then offer Him your love in the many ways He inspires you. Close with a prayer from Scripture.

End your prayers while reflecting on Scripture with a resolution that is related to the virtues by which you would like to live the fullness of your Christian life. Plan what virtues appeal to you.

Read the Psalms prayerfully. Select the different types in keeping with your desires at the time such as those on praise, thanksgiving, sorrow, petition. Read slowly and only a few verses. Select those verses that speak directly to you and meditate on each thought.

Continue to read the Psalms for both morning and evening prayer for a certain period until they become part of you as they did when they were sung by those who walked the earth waiting for Christ to come. Meditate on them in relation to your own needs or moods at that time.

Prepare to enter into the Mass of the next day prayerfully by reading the Scripture and other prayers. This will make a great difference in your participation.

Read the Sermon on the Mount and the spiritual and

corporal works of mercy. Develop each into a prayer asking that you live these mandates in your spiritual life so you will grow in Christ.

Plan for the reception of Holy Communion and make your thanksgiving after by meditating on the gifts of the Holy Spirit and the virtues which lend themselves to prayers for they include all needs as you address them to the Holy Spirit and ask Him to intercede with the Father for you.

Open the Scripture to any quotation during the day and address it as a prayer to God the Father and you will be surprised how you will grow in prayer for God is directing you as He speaks to you.

Read during October the different selections in Scripture related to the mysteries of the rosary. Make a meditation. Pray for the needs of different people and ask for certain virtues.

Go with Christ to the cross on Calvary where He gave His last sermon. Listen to Him speak to you now and pray these farewell prayers by applying them to your own life.

Select Scripture readings that lend themselves to meeting Christ in the Blessed Sacrament and develop a Holy Hour, a visit to the Blessed Sacrament, a Scripture Service.

Many of the suggested activities included for each year in the chapter on prayer could be included in this program, which could be used as a review, or part of a day of recollection or an evening retreat where prayer would be the theme. These activities could be directed toward the relationship of prayer to Scripture and the different ways students need to be involved in prayer as it is stressed in the curriculum.

Developing a Spiritual Life Style through Scripture

The reading of Scripture will help youth develop their own life style as they reflect on the message. Youth hungers for the spiritual. Concentrating on definite activities that are Christ-centered and related to Christ-likeness will enrich the lives of youth as they acquire those virtues that will enable them to be influential apostles. Christ gave many mandates as He walked His way along the path of life that could be applied to these modern times. As youth are given directives in reflecting on these, they will take on personalities that influence, they will be able to love, and will be instruments in bringing Christ's message to the world. Here are some:

Develop into meditations or prayers selections from Scripture that relate to those virtues that contribute to the personality of the students such as faith, hope, love, prayer, compassion, humility, patience, accepting God's will. Follow by making brief acts of adoration, sorrow, praise, or petitions for different graces. Could be taped and played in class. Introduce and conclude with lines of poetry or song related to the themes being considered.

Try to understand the different types of people one must live with or work with. See Christ in them and meditate on how to accept, respect them, even love them, and go out to them if need be. Consider: people who have harmed you, those who annoy you, those who need you, such as the sick, the poor, the unhappy, the old, the lonely, the alienated, prisoners, the unwanted. Add your own to this list.

What plan do you have to include these people in your prayers? Are there others that you should keep in mind who depend upon you for help in prayer? Reflect on Christ's presence in connection with this reaction to people and to the events of life.

Go through Scripture and select the commands that God gave us, such as love your enemies; judge not and you will not be judged, etc. What do these recommendations mean to you? What could you do about living in keeping with what they ask? Conduct a brief discussion with the class. Have a student leader determine how one should really live these.

Have students bring records with a message. Change the lyrics of the song by replacing them with parts of Scripture.

Ask students to develop a plan of life based upon Scripture

that they could live by. Such would contribute to their maturity and give them that needed confidence. They could develop by considering:

Five personal goals by which they could live and should be part of.

Five values that could become convictions.

Five problems that they should learn to live with if they want to follow Christ.

Five responsibilities which they should accept if they are really Christians.

Five weaknesses that they should avoid.

Five virtues they could acquire that would improve their personality, especially if they feel at times they are unwanted and not loved.

This would take time and the teacher would have to help so that they would select what is possible. Give illustrations to life situations. At an exchange session all members of the class would have ideas to consider regarding their own growth as persons.

Question youth on their acceptance of Scripture and their reactions to reading it on their own.

Continue this assignment by having the class give ways the reading of Scripture could be more widely used by Catholic young adults so they will come to realize that Christ speaks to them in Scripture. Draw conclusions on what could be done in your class, among other Catholic students.

Mini-Retreats, Evenings of Recollection

Closely allied to the spiritual life style that the reading of Scripture will encourage are spiritual renewal programs that lend themselves to evenings of recollection, sometimes called mini-retreats. These retreat programs have taken on new and different ways from the silent longer retreat of earlier times. Students often prepare these retreats with the directors, and participate in the varying types of programs. They also sponsor retreats if they are involved in youth ministries, in teaching religion, or leading discussion groups among young adults.

These evenings of recollection which last about three or four hours after school offer small groups spiritual renewed programs for different classes or clubs on the Catholic high school campus. They are also open to guests, students might invite and sometimes to their parents as father and son, or mother and daughter retreats, and at times all members of the family elect to participate in these evenings of recollection.

Appoint a committee to prepare the details such as the singing, the Mass participation, the prayers of the faithful, the communal penance service, the readings, and leaders for the different prayers. These evenings of retreat do not have to follow the same programs. There are so many ways the activities contribute to the deepening of the spiritual life. Short periods of special involvements in the things that youth enjoy are effective in forming Catholics who have a deep appreciation of their faith and are growing in apostolic zeal. The priest or priests are there to direct the activities, assisted by other faculty members, while allowing students to lead when prepared. Mass is offered and confessions heard. Supper is provided by students bringing the different items while another committee is responsible for seeing to the details. Expense is minimal.

The spiritual renewal programs that students could sponsor come in many packaged forms. They are complete in themselves for immediate presentation with parts being omitted, additions included, and different activities combined. They are flexible and lend themselves to the spiritual development of youth in keeping with their age and maturity. Some of the following themes offer the busy teacher *Instant Spiritual Renewal Programs* for these mini-retreats:

For Meeting Christ in Our Lives, select: Coming to Christ, Discovering Christ, Meeting Christ. Walking with Christ, Growing in Christ. Becoming a Complete Person in Christ as Friends of Christ. Meeting Christ through Lives of Prayer.

Coming to Know Christ in the Blessed Sacrament. Encountering Christ in the Sacraments. Christ Answers the Problems of These Times. Seeing Christ in Others, in the Events of the Day.

For Spiritual Renewal Programs based on Searching, select: Man's Search for Meaning. Quest, A Search for Identity. Discovery and the New Generation. Social Concerns and the Youth Revolution. Living as Christians.

For Spiritual Renewal Programs Based on Facing Moral Problems, select: Moral Problems and Human Dignity. Meeting Death and Eternal Life. Orientation Begins Now for a Happy Marriage. Conflicts in Faith and Faith Experiences. Meeting Life's Problems with a Personal Philosophy.

Within this program are to be found prayer activities that could be used in developing the prayer life of these high school students and in shared prayer which is so popular. Many of the ideas that offer *instant programs* can become part of some of the choices that students make in selecting involvements in preparation for class assignments. They are excellent in creating the climate for students entering into an evening of recollection. This is essential because of the short time required for these spiritual life styles that are being encouraged.

The guidelines that are incorporated into the packaged programs make it easy for students to sponsor these activities without too much effort as they try to involve all their classmates to assure participation as opposed to passiveness which too frequently takes place when they just listen to a lecture.

Reading Scripture Daily After Graduation

Students' study of the Word should not end with the close of the semester. The teaching of Scripture should be so dynamic that youth will continue reading it long after graduation. They are then more likely to make the reading and reflecting on the Word an integral part of the prayer life in the homes they will some day establish.

The different activities in which youth have been involved during their consideration of Scripture will offer them ideas to pursue in depth later. They have been encouraged to choose their readings, to make their own decisions in the application of same, and to assume responsibility for the enriching of their personal spiritual life. They have come to realize how Christ speaks directly to them in Scripture. They were motivated to cultivate their own prayer life. As time moves along they will select those other activities in keeping with those longings which are part of each one.

The directives which follow will enable these students to participate intelligently in the prayer and Scripture groups that are increasing as people gather together to pray everywhere. Or they can be used to bring the power of the Word to those who have not had the same educational experiences.

Set aside a time to reflect on Scripture. At first it might be only 15 minutes. After a while, you will spend more time. If you are rushed, take just one thought for that day and reflect on it along the way.

Follow whatever plan appeals to you. Keep to this plan until you feel you need a change. This will help you develop self-discipline. Never allow it to become mere routine. Take different approaches to reflect on the varying passages. Remember God walks with you and you with God. He is working through you.

Change the activity for praying as you change the passages. Try to be alert and alive to the God who is directing you. Sharing is helpful to some people. You might even start your own small groups and grow in God's love through the exchange of ideas.

Students should plan their own program for reading Scripture each day so that they can continue to grow in Christ long after they have left the halls of their high school. Faith needs constant nourishment and youth needs to be given ideas how to live and grow with faith. They could choose Scripture quotations that have a particular appeal. That is why choice should enter into their different assignments so that they will know why they like something, or even why they are tired of it at a particular time. Or, they could follow the liturgical year and select those sections that refer to the life of Christ from the announcement of His coming, through Advent, Christmas, and into Lent, on to the great day of Pentecost when the Holy Spirit came down on the first apostles.

At other times, these teenagers could be exposed to a climate that they would choose to concentrate on those readings that give an account of Christ's miracles, the parables by which He taught us, or any one of the quotations that would have a special message for them at that time. If, at first they were faithful to reading and reflecting on Scripture for three to ten minutes each day, later they would choose to continue for twenty or thirty minutes. For those who enter into meditating on Scripture and seeing the relationship of what Christ said when He walked the earth to these times, will come to enjoy this religious experience every day. Exposed to the study of Scripture, they will acquire a "know how" and will really want this encounter with Christ, and depend upon Him who is their strength and their hope.

Today, more people have opportunities for advanced education and for spiritual development through the sacraments, daily Mass, and days of recollection so they have been prepared to assist the priests in the work of the Church in its many ministries. For that reason, Catholic schools must offer programs that will make such training possible as encouraged in the decrees of Vatican II.

CHAPTER SIX

TRAINING YOUNG EVANGELISTS

Catholic educators with vision encourage long-time planning to prepare youth in our Catholic schools through training programs to teach religion classes once a week. They are the teachers of tomorrow so should be exposed to professional courses that they might bring the Good News to those who are not attending Catholic schools. Then, when they have their own families, they will know how to teach and form their own children according to Christ's recommendations.

As religious teachers continue to decrease in numbers and withdraw from Catholic schools, the laity will play a more important part in instructing these children. Our Catholic people have been generous in volunteering their services to teach religion even though they were not trained. This has not been an ideal situation. Provision must be made for more effective programs if these children are to be taught about Christ and what He expects of them by professionally trained teachers.

True, CCD programs are highly organized on paper; much money has been spent on the attractive series of books, audio visual materials, and guidelines that unprepared teachers were able to use to advantage. Even with the aid of mini-courses, packaged programs, and teachers' manuals, students were not reached. The drop-out from classes causes great alarm to the pastors. They need help and Catholic education must make such possible.

Realistic religion programs must be organized and incorporated into the religion offerings of the future. Religious studies offered at the college level are among the popular majors for both Catholic and non-Catholic universities. Such must enter the Catholic high school with the present emphasis upon the Youth Ministry. The Catholic high school offers an ideal place to train religion teachers who could get their start under supervision during these formative years and while volunteer services are encouraged. One day a week in every religion class at every level, students should be trained on how to teach religion, first to the younger students, and later to the older ones.

Develop a sequence of classes with a curriculum outline that will include content, experiences, activities, opportunities for observation, and teaching under supervision, until they are able to go on their own. Students will begin as teacher helpers, and will learn how to prepare materials, run AV equipment related to the lessons. Such training will enable them to be effective teachers for the parishes of tomorrow.

Catholic high schools have the responsibility to serve the communities where they are located. They must provide those programs that will assist the church of today and tomorrow. Much emphasis is placed in establishing Christian communities and communities of faith which tend to be superficial in their present organization. They need a definite purpose and from such will come real and genuine communities where people are able to work and pray together as they prepare for bringing Christ to these children. Being active in religion training programs demands prayer and sacrifice for success, and will give a certain style to any community that naturally follows. Such a community would have substance and contribute to the formation of the individual as a mature person, a Christian, and an effective teacher of religion.

Evangelization Requires Organization

The religion coordinator of the high school should appoint at each class level a teacher to organize a program for training youth once a week within the regular religion classes. True, some students might never teach, but time would not be wasted, for the classes should offer dynamic challenges. They will learn how to teach, as they are involved in teaching. Such will prepare them to train their own children, to form them in Christ, and to participate in the parish programs that will need their services in the years ahead.

Evangelization is related to this youth ministry. The pilot study within the regular religion classes will train these young people to work with their peers. They will be ideal to teach even younger boys and girls if effectively trained to bring the teachings of Christ to these little ones.

Evangelization not only includes teaching but it asks youth to go out to those who know not Christ, to bring about conversations among those young teenagers who have fallen away from the faith, to make the contacts and offer them ways to return to God. As youth becomes activated through the youth ministries they will be most effective through prayer and their apostolic involvments in making those contacts that will enable them to know about, and choose to participate in, the religion in which they were baptized. Think of the large numbers who will come to God if each one in religion classes went out to one and invited him to attend religion classes or programs that he would enjoy so he would come to Christ as is His plan.

In the programs which follow will be found ideas that will enable students in the religion classes to prepare for teaching and the other involvement activities related to the youth ministries:

Contact youth whose parents are divorced and have neglected their religion training, or the fallen-away Catholics who neglect the spiritual formation of their sons and daughters. They need to make this person-to-person contact.

Form small prayer groups, or Scripture study programs for high school youth on their block which would draw many Catholics who have little knowledge of their faith.

Sponsor dramatic productions, or choir rehearsals. They

should be open to teenagers and the Catholic students could accompany those who would like to participate in these activities and thus many more will come to know Christ.

Attend Mass with another teenager and help him to participate in the Mass intelligently and prayerfully. Explain the meaning of the Mass which should lead to further instructions.

Offer spiritual renewal programs in many different places in the form of mini-retreats or evenings of recollection. Youth who have been negligent about their religion could be invited and accompanied by another which might be the start of his return to God.

Recommend books, recordings, and cassettes that these students who really do not know Christ would enjoy and such might open avenues that would lead them back to God. Invite them over some evening with other Catholic friends to listen and talk.

These limited ideas are a way to contact others. Those students who are apostolic and concerned about evangelization will find other programs to participate in with a few fallen-away Catholics or the poorly instructed. They are just waiting for someone to invite them to an activity which will enable them to realize their responsibilities to God. Students could pray that such contacts will be made. Those of other faiths are aggressive, yet most successful, as they invite people they meet at the beaches or other vacation places to read Scripture and to attend their centers. With encouragement, comparable programs will be explained in our schools, and in keeping with God's plan, many Catholic teenagers will choose to pursue these people and bring them to Christ.

Objectives of the Youth Ministry:

1. To prepare youth to teach religion while in high school and to offer them realistic experiences:

At the high school grade level in which they are enrolled through a once-a-week program within the regular religion class. They will serve in their own parish or others who need their volunteer services in teaching the grade school students attending public schools This program will give them knowledge and training that will enable them to form their own children in keeping with God's teachings and His plan of salvation.

2. To involve Catholic high school youth in the teaching of religion, that is:

To review basic doctrines of their religion in a meaningful way. Such will assure more intelligent Catholics.

To become active in the Youth Ministry suggested by the Bishops in recent publications on the teaching of religion, especially *To Teach as Jesus Did*.

To participate in creating innovative religion programs that will make Christ more personal to them.

3. To serve the Catholic community. In large Catholic high schools, 30 or more parishes send their children to the secondary school. These students:

Should volunteer their services while being trained in their own parishes.

Should participate in promoting the Liturgy. Should become active in the choir so they can add to the beauty of liturgical worship.

4. To cooperate with priests of the parish in carrying out the purpose of Catholic education in preparing Catholic leaders who will activate this or a comparable program in whatever parish they establish their own homes. Such a program:

Will provide a large pool of trained people to bring Christ to youth as they communicate effectively with these young people.

Will up-grade the religion offerings and will attract a larger number of better prepared teachers who will be effective in forming youth.

Will enable teachers to offer varying and enriching

programs that will continue students' spiritual development.

5. To unite parishes and the high schools as a supportive effort through this involvement program. It will require priests in the parish, and the teachers who coordinate the program to work with these students as they train them and:

Provide opportunities for teaching religion, first through observation, then through participation in preparation, and finally through actually teaching.

Offer these young adults spiritual renewal programs as they teach classes of young children that they might be prepared spiritually.

Enable youth to develop a Christ-like life and thus deepen their own faith and that of those they influence.

Make possible future Catholic homes through this involvement in teaching religion in keeping with the liturgical year.

6. To enable Catholic high school graduates to be effectively prepared:

To enroll in Catholic colleges and State universities offering a major in Religious Studies.

To inspire more students to become young evangelists for the Catholic faith and to work among youth in foreign countries.

To offer youth an educational, spiritual, and liturgical program in keeping with the innovations that are growing and the personnel involved:

Lectors who can really proclaim Scripture when reading at Mass.

Deacons who will take the professional and spiritual training required to be ordained as such.

Extraordinary ministers as more Catholics are assigned to bring Holy Communion to the sick in hospitals and convalescent homes, and to distribute the Eucharist at Masses.

Lay missioners in distant lands to serve the Third

World for short periods of time.

Religious. More youth might come to appreciate the life because of the varying involvements in the teaching of religion.

Priests. Boys in larger number are more likely to answer the call of God to be priests.

The courses would train students for on-going experiences in this once-a-week religion class. At the end of four years these students would have met the requirements that would include:

Content offered at different class levels from grades 1 to 8, or 1 to 6, and 8 to 10, and some cases 11 and 12.

Books used at each level along with the Teacher Manuals and guide lines that are needed in teaching.

Techniques for teaching such as class management, use of AV materials, telling stories, teaching singing, preparing students for the Sacraments, the Liturgy, and comparable experiences.

Teacher-helpers learning how to teach and to work with small groups.

Observation of classes under direction so they will become aware of working with students and relating to youth at different ages.

Supervision of their teaching under trained supervisors.

Experience in classes when ready to take over the different levels.

Teacher-training certificates should be presented to seniors at the end of their four years of training if they have met the requirements. Such a program would assure a large number of professionally prepared teachers to bring the Good News to their own children in the years ahead, to offer their services during their college days or while working after graduation, to teach religion in their own parishes in keeping with the mandates of Vatican II as stated in the *Church and the Modern World*.

Begin now with this or a comparable training program in every

Catholic high school. If those not of our faith can train their youth to be effective Sunday school teachers, why not Catholic educators? We must save our children, too frequently turned off in the present once-a-week classes for public school youth because of the inexperience of their teachers. These students are entitled to a knowledge of Christ, in a way that they will want to love Him and serve Him.

To organize a teacher-training program within religion classes should not be left to chance. It will demand time and effort as the creative leader brings to this program challenging ideas. It offers an answer to those Catholic educators who advocate that religion be taught only four times a week and to those educators who are looking for volunteer experiences for their Christian Social Service programs which require students to donate 100 to 200 hours a year to dedicated services. It will provide that spiritual development for which youth hunger and which concerns religion teachers.

Evangelization Requires Varying Experiences

To have an effective program, the religion department must develop its own syllabus for each class level. During the first years, consider it experimental, revising it each year in keeping with the findings from evaluations conducted by students and teachers. In time, student representatives should be on the committees who will work out a four year program.

The training in this once-a-week class should follow the laboratory approach for the program will necessitate the securing of materials for each class to be taught. A resource center could be established so students would have access to books and aids that would assist them in preparing lessons which would provide experiences through the grades. Students could work in teams to demonstrate and conduct programs such as:

Telling stories at the lower grade level. These students could circulate in several different classes once they have mastered several stories that will illustrate a doctrine of faith.

Teaching singing at the different grade levels. They should learn how to train small groups for singing before being assigned to train choirs.

Playing the organ or the guitar. See that students have training in these instruments if they are capable of doing so. Engage a master teacher if necessary. The Church is entitled to well-prepared music.

Leading discussions. Students should be trained in their regular religion classes. They should be given small groups to teach according to this method of learning.

Organizing para-liturgical programs for important feasts or communal penance services. This training should be part of the regular religion offerings so let those of ability demonstrate by presenting such programs to these once-a-week religion classes.

Preparing liturgical programs that will make the Mass more meaningful. If students are well prepared in their religion classes, with a little work they can instruct these students in an appreciation and love of the Mass.

Planning prayer programs of different types that will involve youth in shared prayer experiences, especially those related to Scripture, to meditation, to reflection.

The Catholic high school will work with the priests of the parish, and with the lay people in charge as students are given their assignments at the different class levels. Each group can contribute to the effectiveness of the program as it is worked out with the school and the parish. If the diocese has special outlines for CCD classes, they will have to be followed. There should be a high degree of flexibility at first which would allow for adaptation in keeping with the needs and the types of students being taught.

Organize the religion training program in keeping with the age level in which students will be involved in teaching. As youths are trained for the doctrine to be presented, they must consider the teaching techniques that are related. Students need varying experiences which will prepare them for observation and supervised teaching. Evaluate with students the different steps that must be followed so that they will grow in confidence and be effective teachers.

Students who are to teach must learn to depend upon God for students and must be trained to pray to be instruments that they will be able to bring the Good News to those entrusted to them. The more youth see their place in carrying out God's plan for salvation, the more likely they are to learn how they must call on Him if they are to enjoy success. Prayer vigils, twilight retreats and comparable religious experiences will enrich the lives of these student-teachers as they enter a classroom to bring Christ's love and concern to these young children.

Students need to be exposed to the total program, the principles, and procedures which are part of class presentation such as (1) the objectives for teaching religion, (2) the psychological principles that must be included, and (3) the teaching procedures that will be effective. These might be taught when students are ready to actually teach. During the days of preparation as teacher helpers and observers, they will indirectly become aware of these basic learning techniques.

Objectives in Teaching Religion

The listed objectives are general in nature and the training teacher should consider with these student-teachers ways in which they could implement them as they present them in their classes. They should be incorporated into their actual teaching as they prepare a plan to evaluate how their students are growing in the knowledge and love of Christ through the varying doctrines taught:

To come to know Christ personally.

To really love Christ as they take on His ways.

To serve Him which He asks of all Christians.

To study His teachings in keeping with the plan He gave us in Scripture as directed by His Church.

To deepen their spiritual life through prayer and the Sacraments.

To respect themselves as persons with God-given dignities.

To consider one's life by giving of oneself.

To be Christian witnesses for Christ.

As these student-teachers enter the classroom, they are likely to make these objectives more concrete as they work with youth and consider their personal goals and sense of values. If students know where they are going, what is expected of them, they will become aware of God's personal plan and loving concern for each of them.

Psychological Principles in Teaching Religion

Students in training need to be exposed to basic psychological principles that will enable them to direct the learning activities of the class. The following are briefly stated and will need a more in-depth presentation:

To learn how to observe, to become aware in seeing and hearing.

To associate what is being taught or considered with the past or previous learning experiences.

To relate to the present, to the past, to something different, but especially to here and now in the application.

To learn how to listen attentively.

To teach concepts rather than mere facts when possible.

To provide those learning experiences that will enable students to:

Follow directives intelligently.

Assimilate materials by overlearning.

Confirm what they read or learn through repeating, or re-reading.

Understand what is expected in a given assignment.

Question intelligently.

Make application to life here and now.
Draw conclusions based on facts and not rumor or opinion.
Widen their horizons through independent study.
Open new avenues through enriching experiences.
Become involved in intelligent discussions.
Be responsible for their personal development as Christians.

Teaching Procedures in Studying Religion

Student teachers will see a relationship to psychological principles as well as teaching procedures as they are being trained. It is difficult to see the difference at times for they are both part of the details that enter into the preparation that will enable the student teachers to instruct youth:
To select the materials and activities needed to present and teach a definite lesson.
To illustrate for their class how to go about studying.
To review with students.
To vary the lesson.
To work with small groups.
To inspire students through readings, illustrations, and the arts.
To challenge students through the different types of assignments.
To provide enriching experiences for the more intelligent.
To evaluate their own teaching.
To learn how to evaluate the students by following definite grading procedures.
To learn how to make lesson plans.
To follow the directives given by the master teacher until they are on their own.

Routine Responsibilities for Teachers

The teaching of religion will be more effective if those in

training are exposed and made to assume responsibility for the routines that contribute to the learning process and class discipline. These routines should be part of the professional training of these young students. Many of them they would have learned as teacher-helpers or during their observation assignments.

Keep the roll book as is expected.

Record the grades for the teacher.

See that the room is in order at the end of the class.

Change the bulletin boards.

Assume responsibility for securing and distributing the books, papers, and materials needed by the students.

In addition to taking care of these routine activities, the student teacher should also assume responsibilities directly related to the learning process:

Take charge of the class while the teacher is busy or out for a short period of time. Continue the teaching procedure or supervise the students. Walk around to see that they are working.

Work with small groups who are preparing an assignment. Locate materials that are needed. Help them with discussion techniques. Keep them on the topic.

Accompany small groups to the church for a liturgical service, to the library to secure books, on a field trip that has been approved.

Supervise a group or class who are viewing the film. Follow with a discussion so they will see the relationship to the subject at hand.

See that all types of AV materials are ready if the class is going to be involved in any form of the media, including filmstrips and recordings.

Learn how to involve all students in discussion or in class assignments, especially those who are extremely shy and need encouragement. Watch that the aggressive ones do not dominate.

Direct the singing, prepare the words, go over the Liturgy

so students will grow in understanding and will participate in the different programs.

Go over the assignments after the teachers have presented them so that students will understand what is required.

With our high school students being exposed to training, they will be able to take over classes under supervision and later on their own.

These religion programs can become part of the curriculum immediately. All that is needed are people with vision and apostolic zeal who will dare to start and carry out such a simple program. Truly, the Church will have entered into a form of evangelization that will prepare a large pool of teachers for the immediate future. This was the concern of the Synod of Bishops who met in Rome a decade after the close of Vatican II when they considered the need for evangelization programs which are now being talked about.

There will then be a Youth Ministry which will grow and take on many different forms as advocated so strongly in the document *To Teach as Jesus Did*. Begin by activating the junior groups who need youth sponsors with creative ideas such as the Legion of Mary and the Theresians. Catholic educators indeed make a contribution if they would sponsor programs that are different as they provide religious experiences that involve youth.

SUGGESTED TEACHING ASSIGNMENTS

For Ninth Grade Students

Act as helpers to teachers at first and second grade levels.

Work with small groups after learning how to observe.

Teach prayers in chorus, than individually.

Tell students stories, especially about the Saints.

Follow the liturgical year in their explanation as related to their age and as found in books.

Train in brief songs.
Use records and cassettes to illustrate.
Present film strips related to the content.

For Tenth Grade Students

Continue the same types of assignments and experiences as outlined for the ninth grade, using different content.
Help prepare for first confession, first Holy Communion.
Teach additional prayers, songs, stories.
Work with small groups at first.
Take over the class under supervision when needed.
Assist the teacher in the details, gathering the required materials.
See that you have experiences in AV presentations of all types.

For Eleventh Grade Students

Assignments should be made in keeping with their previous experiences and their abilities. Many students could do more advanced work. They should be assigned to the program for shorter periods such as four and six week sessions.

Consider the program for fifth and sixth grade students. For junior high school, if divided that way, which would include seventh, eighth and ninth grade. For the middle schools which would include grades 6, 7, 8, 9 or grades 7, 8, 9, 10.

Be sure that they have different offerings and are well planned in order to challenge the students at these grades. See that the students understand the content presented, have the materials needed, are prepared through observation. Include varying techniques to involve the students. Work under supervision with master teachers. Evaluate their teaching after each lesson. See that they are given advanced seminars for teaching.

For Twelfth Grade Students

If these students have followed the regular teacher training program for three years and have been involved in teaching, those of ability are ready for experiences even at the 10th, 11th, or 12th grade levels. They should be challenged to take on different assignments. Those with special talents such as music should be involved in these ministries and receive advanced training while teaching youth. Enriching assignments would encourage them to continue teaching after they enroll in college. Some of the following could be considered:

Training other students at the lower class levels. Supervising their teaching, the music, the paraliturgical programs, etc.

Conducting small seminars at the peer level on Scripture such as The Acts of the Apostles, the Gospels, the Epistles of St. Paul.

Directing Catholic reading programs such as following the great books techniques from the 7th through the 12th grade.

Preparing Confirmation classes completely. Seeing that students realize the importance of the Holy Spirit in their lives.

Planning retreats for students of different age levels.

Teaching class by the use of films, filmstrips, etc.

As high school students are exposed to the new dimensions in these training programs their religion will be appreciated and they are likely to see its relationship to life as they bring the Good News to others. This combined program of being involved in advanced studies of religion while learning how to teach religion to younger students should offer youth an excellent review while deepening their knowledge and love for God.

Retreats, Evenings of Recollection

Generally, a student committee organizes the activities for

these spiritual programs. They provide excellent opportunities for training in leadership as these teenagers are effective in influencing their peers and this is an ideal way to do so.

The suggested retreat involvements could be used in these evenings of recollection which begin shortly after the end of school, around four o'clock and continue on to nine or ten o'clock. They could be adapted to:

Mini-retreats in parishes on Saturdays or Sundays for all the youth of the parish.

Religious renewal programs for public school students who attend the once-a-week religion classes.

Week-end retreats away from the school in a mountain resort where youth could gather.

The students who have been trained at school could organize and train other youth in this excellent apostolic activity that will contribute to their spiritual growth.

There are many different ways that students could be involved in these dynamic programs. The committee could determine the agenda and the time for each activity. Also, they should plan the publicity, and if it is by invitation, they should issue same. After each evening of recollection, have students complete a brief evaluation sheet. This will enable the committee to consider the recommendations and make the changes needed.

Retreat Activities

The committee should assign two students to be responsible for each phase of the retreat. They should understand their assignments and should be creative in their presentations. Teenagers must be involved under the direction of their leaders who should prepare worthwhile involvements.

The retreat could open with a conference. As youth are more concerned about their own spiritual life, the share-exchange activity offers them the needed observations and evaluations which enable them to relate their longings to their daily life style. Student leaders must be prepared to lead this activity while the priests and faculty members act as consultants.

The share-exchange activity could include the entire group of 40 to 50 students, even more. Or the retreatants might be divided into groups of ten or twelve students. They could report their conclusions at the close of this session so all could benefit from their considerations.

Share-Exchange Activities

Through these exchanges, youth will come to know that others have the same concerns and problems. Great strength will come to one another through the inspiration and courage manifested in witnessing to the obstacles they or others have had to face, and the sacrifices they have made.

Select a theme for this sharing or develop these exchanges around the one chosen for the retreat. Leaders need to prepare the involvement activities or questions so that the observations made, and the experiences given, will have substance. It might take time to develop worthwhile problems for the teenagers to attack. They could be listed and duplicated and students would choose as a group the ones they would like to consider. Or they could be typed and cut. Then the student could take one from a box and would present it to the group giving his own experiences or asking the group to share comparable ones related to the topic.

Ask students to give observations of the incident or problem in the shared exchange. It could be from real life or from a book read, or a TV program. They should describe the incident in detail which would lead to questioning, to personal application in their own lives, and make recommendations for the future. The theme of the consideration could be presented from any vantage point, and developed. Here are a few that lend themselves to this program of shared activities:

Prayer in the life of a teenager.
Prayer in the life of a Christian.
Reading Scripture. What does it mean to you? Why?

Faith. Do you have it? How can it be nurtured?
Virtues. Cover certain ones. Be definite in application.
Beatitudes. Christ asks us to live in keeping with these recommendations. How?
The Mass. What do you get out of it? What do you give? Why is it important?
The Blessed Sacrament. Why do so many receive Holy Communion, while so few make visits?
Problems of teenagers.

It would be effective to begin with their own experiences in keeping with the topic chosen for consideration. Then, have them make observations to show how others have lived in keeping with the idea developed. Move along by asking questions that will require other incidents and observations. Encourage personal reactions. Students can disagree. They might need direction so they can relate to their own lives. Give time to silently making a personal commitment. Conclude with a prayer asking for God's grace to live what they have decided should be their plan for spiritual growth.

Now and again, the last part of this shared-exchange could be a meditation with students giving their own thoughts in keeping with the theme, or prayer readings that are related could be read in that they are beautiful and inspirational. Allow time for silence. Another activity could be reading Scripture, with prayers in between, which could be silent or aloud. Use the different Psalms for they have a special message, or read from Scripture the sections on the Mysteries of the Rosary as they are the basic doctrines by which Christians live. Also the Seven Last Words from the Cross offer ideal meditations that challenge modern youth.

Evaluation of the Mini-Retreat

Here are a few questions that could be used to evaluate the retreat. Have them prepared and allow time at the close for students to complete. They do not need to sign their names. Substitute more related questions. Conduct a follow-up to decide what changes are of value in keeping with their suggestions. Leave space on the duplicated sheet to write their answers. Your own observations will see other needs.

What did I expect from this evening of recollection? Did what I expected enter into the retreat?

What changes did this spiritual renewal program make in my life?

What parts of this program did I like and would recommend to continue? Why?

What recommendations would I make that would improve the program?

Consider what should not be continued, and offer other ideas that you think teenagers would enjoy.

Enriching Experiences Activate Youth Ministries

Closely allied to the youth ministries are those experiences that they could plan with their peers where they would be of service to people who would benefit from their leadership and would involve them in activities that would be enriching for them personally as they reach out to others, especially the disadvantaged. They would be bringing Christ to others if they would organize programs that would enable them to work with youth from broken homes, with retarded children, with emotionally disturbed boys and girls, with those who are neglected by their parents because they work or are indifferent to their needs. Some of the following activities lend themselves to ministry on a one-to-one basis or at least in small groups:

Take a disadvantaged youth to visit an art center, a museum, a shopping center, a theater, a park, a playground, a bank, a post office, a factory, a mission, a church. There are other places that could be chosen.

Select a place to visit that does not cost, like a beach, a park, a mountain, etc. Bring a book to read to these children so that they will enjoy a story, a poem, something beautiful that they do not generally experience.

Spend some time with emotionally disturbed children if such is possible. Often all they need is love, people to care for them by playing with or listening to them.

Play with crippled or deformed children if there is a children's hospital near by. Encourage your class companions to make things and bring them to these children. They enjoy simple things.

Direct drama programs, art classes, poetry-readings for disadvantaged children during the summer. Or play records, teach them songs, and enable them to do things on their own so they will not become juvenile delinquents.

Create a film festival for youth of a particular age. You can obtain free films from the local library.

Organize song-fests and teach children how to sing. Even organize a choir for your parish church for the smaller children. You develop your leadership qualities as you go out to others.

Donate time to teach swimming, to teach games in any form, to be a life guard so children can enjoy a pool. Instruct these students in first aid.

Develop a baby-sitting club, offer services without charge for one or two hours each week to a busy mother who cannot afford such and needs a rest or time to do something.

Accompany teenagers from broken homes or from homes where the faith is not practiced to Mass on Sunday or to the school of religion that is held once a week in all parishes. Often, they are afraid to go alone.

Form a Scripture study group for students who do not go to Catholic schools. Keep it just for about four weeks unless youth shows great interest to continue.

Offer your services to a blind organization. If you have a good voice, help them to make cassettes on articles, or chapters from books. Accompany a blind person.

Become an active member in the junior Legion of Mary or

the junior Theresians. These programs will enable you to grow spiritually and within them you will find opportunities as you go out to people to include some of these ideas that have been suggested.

The youth ministries encourage this one-to-one basis of working with youth, or the small groups organizing programs that are needed. Too frequently, planned programs fail because they involve too many and they are not consistent in following any assignment through. With a few students responsible for different types of activities, they are likely to be more successful. The training that would enter into the preparation of these apostolic activities would contribute to the maturity of youth as they share in the formation and happiness of others.

The youth ministries offer many outlets for zealous students with talents and abilities. They need to be encouraged and directed in reaching out to other youth. This is a growing movement that will offer the teenagers of today the challenges for which they are looking.

Creative ideas will continue to enrich and contribute to the evangelization of youth by youth. So many young people were lost to the church during the Sixties due to the confusion of those times, and also to the neglect of parents in some cases. Now new vistas are opening within the youth ministries as they bring the teachings of Christ, often in an indirect manner, to those who hunger for the spiritual.

CHAPTER SEVEN

COMMITMENT, A CALL TO DISCIPLESHIP WITH CHRIST

Every man is called by God to a particular vocation to a definite commitment, to be His disciple in carrying out His work, in accepting His will as he walks in time with a definite purpose towards eternity. God has a divine plan for each person whereby each one, if he cooperates, will reach his potential spirituality. This call to holiness is for all people, not for a select few. Christ in His directives asks everyone to live the Gospel values, to develop a life of prayer, make sacrifices, and to give of themselves in loving service. Youth must be informed how to answer Christ's call, to follow his vocation either in the lay apostolate, or in the religious life, or in the priesthood.

Those youth who claim they are in search for identity will find it in Christ. They need to understand His call to discipleship that they might respond. The longing for fulfillment for which they cry, will only be found in eternity when they are with Christ. This should be made clear to them. In the meantime, they will be prepared for this union with Christ through the involvements that prayer and sacrifice demand in keeping with their commitments. Students are searching. So the religion curriculum should offer programs that will be both informative and inspirational in keeping with these longings. They need either a unit of study or once-a-year program to understand and appreciate the work of the laity who have a definite place in this call of Christ, and the place of consecrated religious, as well as the priesthood, in the modern world.

Commitment Demands Dedication

Our students have been prepared to a degree for their particular dedication through the study of Scripture, through their activities on prayer, and through their exposure to the newer movements. The age of spiritual renewal and reconciliation has opened many different life styles for youth, who need though, a deeper understanding of the place of consecrated religious and priests in the plan of God. This form of the spiritual life has been neglected during the past decade. New programs are being developed by religious communities to make young adults aware of the varying apostolates. Christ continues to call people to follow Him through the vows of poverty, chastity, and obedience. Youth must be alerted so that those who are called to this form of commitment will choose to answer Christ's invitation to follow Him in a consecrated life.

Students who have read *To Teach as Jesus Did* know what is being suggested for them to give of themselves for a certain number of hours each week. They know the volunteer programs which are now being required of every high school graduate that they might learn how to be involved in assisting others. They see this call for volunteer services in the secular world, and the invitation to assist in their parishes or communities where people need others. Thus, they are growing in the knowledge that the work of God on earth is truly carried out by those He calls to discipleship with Him.

The educational mission of the Church requires that Catholic education develop zealous apostles, that they develop youth spiritually, and that they expose them to the different ways of establishing and building Christian communities.

To do so, a definite program is needed to challenge youth. The religion department could decide on many approaches that will make students aware of the call of Christ to work in the varying vocations He offers them. It could be:

Once-a-year commitment programs where the call to the lay apostolate and the religious life will be considered during the month of March in honor of St. Joseph, or during May in honor of Our Lady. There are many activities that could involve youth so they can meet the challenges of these times.

Mini-elective or a unit of study which would consider in greater detail how students could serve Christ with special emphasis on the study of the religious life and the priesthood.

Spiritual Renewal Programs that are sponsored by religious communities over week-ends away from school. These are intended to acquaint youth with the different apostolates that are available.

The religion teacher should appoint a committee to work on involvements each year and select the activities that have definite appeal. They should see that materials are available so students can pursue the different types of assignments.

Scripture Readings Related to Vocations

Since Christ calls men to different forms of discipleship as stated in Scripture, it would offer an excellent introduction to read certain selections from Scripture related to the dedication that is required of Christians. In this way, they will come to know Christ's design in calling people in these times to be active lay leaders to bring His teachings to the modern world. Those readings that might more definitely relate to the obligations of the religious life might be included, but could be considered in greater detail later in the study of this form of consecration.

Duplicate the Scripture readings giving chapter and verse so students will read and reflect on their own. Certain readings could be chosen for the different years in high school, or they could be assigned to small groups to develop and share with the entire class. Require the students to read slowly and to apply their message to their relationship with Christ and His call to youth. Direct the discussions so these boys and girls will understand the real meaning that Christ had in mind when He presented His plans for future generations.

Develop the reading assignments around different themes and have students individually or in small groups meditate on these thoughts, applying them to their lives now:

Each person is called to a definite mission in life.
Grow in the Spirit of Christ.
Christian stewardship requires dedicated disciples.
Called to service in this generation.
People need people. Be holy people.
The apostolate of love and service.

Students could change the titles of these suggested themes or develop others. Here are some of the Scripture readings that are related and that would make an excellent preparation in understanding *vocation* as called by Christ.

The Gospel of St. John and his Letters.
Epistles of St. Paul.
Christ's Priestly Prayer before He left the apostles.
Christ's gift of the Holy Eucharist.
Christ at prayer, prayer for all generations.
Luke 12:50, 49, 10:16, 11:28, 12:22, 16:13, 10:16.
Matthew 10:37, 25:14, 13:3, 22:37, 8:20, 18:18, 28:18.
Ephesians 1:3, 1:8, 1:10, 4:15.

Christian Stewardship and Vatican II

Decrees from Vatican II prepare man for that call to discipleship as they recommend plans for growing in holiness in the service of Christ and His Church. Certain selections could be studied in connection with the suggested Scripture readings as they lend themselves to the same themes of stewardship. The following decrees that develop one's leadership abilities are definitely related to the vocation of man to carry Christ's message to the people. Appoint groups to prepare panels and to vary their presentation of the following:

Panel I—The Church in the Modern World. The Apostolate of the Laity.

Panel II—The Missions. Christian Education.

Panel III—Renewal in Religious Life. Priestly Formation. Priest's Ministry.

All members of the class should be required to read these decrees, take notes, and discuss after the presentation by the panelists.

This study should prepare Catholic students to become zealous in proclaiming the Gospel of Christ. Recently a survey stated that the population of Asia was over 21 billion and 65 percent of these people were under 21. Young Christians are traveling far to convert the Asian youth to Christianity and with remarkable success. Our Catholic youth must be inspired to become active in this apostolate. No one knows where Christ calls, where He is leading youth who are concerned about people and their needs. They should be encouraged to serve Christ as volunteers for a period of time. Catholic educators have the responsibility to offer programs that will prepare students for varying forms of discipleship.

Discipleship Now

When the students have considered the call to stewardship, to holiness, to the service of others as reflected in the suggested Scripture and decrees of Vatican II readings, student leaders could develop the following questions in small discussion groups to make this study more realistic, as they apply their findings to living their lives as Catholics here and now. These questions would assist students in creating an effective program:

Show how Vatican II through the teaching of the council connects its recommendations with the call to stewardship in the writings of the apostolate of the laity. Do you think that these decrees need to be implemented to make the laity realize their responsibility? What could be done?

With the gift of faith, does one have to be an apostle? How? Give illustrations of what the laity is doing in the Church today; could do in the future.

Since the purpose of stewardship is to bring man back to God, especially fallen away Catholics, what can the laity of today do to make people realize God's teachings in morals, marriage, business, etc.?

How could Catholic schools show greater leadership in educating Christians to assume responsibility to change the world in keeping with Christ's commands?

What is the relationship of the following terms to discipleship: a pilgrim people, people set apart, a priestly people?

What parables are related to stewardship? Explain this relationship in each one as you apply it to modern life. What different rewards does God give to men?

The call to discipleship expects all baptized Christians to live their lives in keeping with God's plan as revealed in His message. As Catholics identify with Christ they will be faithful to His call and become images of Christ through:

Frequent reception of the Sacraments, especially the Holy Eucharist.

Growth in prayer where the Father through the Holy Spirit speaks to His disciples and reveals Himself through His Son.

Practice of virtues, especially obedience and humility, and the acceptance of His will in the events of life.

Living the Beatitudes which are God's recommendations to those who follow Him.

Reconciliation with others, that is, to forgive, and give of self out of love of God.

A vocation is a call given to each person to carry out the

mission that God has ordained for him to follow. The following titles lend themselves to discussion questions or to essays that could be written after spending some time in study of their meaning and the implementation to life. They could be combined:

Being sent by Christ. Each one has a mission in life.
Call to discipleship. What does that mean to the lay person?
Giving an account of your stewardship. How does it apply?
Gifts are from God to be returned to Him. What are they?
Called to live completely the Christian Life. Why not?
Living your baptismal consecration. What does this mean?
Growing in faith and love. How? Why do Catholics fail?
Having a fruitful Apostolate. What do you plan to do?
Witnessing to Christ at school, in the world.
Living a life of sacrifice and service.
Commitment needs avenues of fulfillment.

The following discussion questions would help teenagers to have an understanding of these themes:

Do you think that many Catholic students understand their call by Christ to serve Him in the world? Why not? What could be done to make them more aware?

How are the Beatitudes related to your consecration or commitment to Christ? Are Catholics aware of living same? Go over each one and illustrate. What ones do you think are neglected by youth? What ones are not understood?

What virtues have you observed in Catholics who frequent the Sacraments weekly? What ones are neglected? Do you think most Catholics realize the power of the Sacraments?

There is an increase in people going to Holy Communion, but fewer people receiving the sacrament of Penance. What would you say is the cause? Have you observed a casualness in dress and reverence in receiving Holy Communion, especially among youth? Why do you think they really understand? Why do people not prepare, not make a thanksgiving? What can be done about it? Relate your attitudes towards being a Christian witness.

Why do people find it difficult to forgive? What can be done to make our teenagers aware of the need of forgiveness? Relate this attitude towards receiving the Sacraments, to death, to judgment, to creating hostilities, to holding grudges, to refusing to speak, to ignoring so-called enemies.

Prepare for Vocation Month a visit to the Blessed Sacrament where students will lead the Rosary and read selected readings. Pray for vocations of different types during the time allowed for spontaneous prayer such as for missioners, for contemplatives, for the priests in their diocese, and for the religious communities that they know or that will be suggested to them.

Organize for another time a procession with songs, recitation of the Rosary for different communities. Visit the shrines on campus and end with a consecration to the Sacred Heart of Jesus. If possible, students could plan an evening candlelight procession and invite their parents. Families should realize their reponsibility for praying for vocations that they might have priests and religious to serve in the decades ahead.

Assign students to prepare a Scripture Service on such themes as: Commitment, The Call of Christ, Christian Witness, Apostolic Involvement, or a comparable title of their choice.

Hold a shared prayer program one day for about 20 minutes. Ask students to select readings, prayers, and incidents on vocations including brief accounts of different communities. Build upon the power of faith and how Christ answers our prayers for He has said, "Ask and you shall receive."

Assign a different student to lead the prayers during this month at the opening of class. Have the student select Scripture readings, verses, or spontaneous prayers related to the vocation needs.

Develop prayers for the faithful that students could use at Mass during the silent time for prayer, in preparation for

Holy Communion, or in thanksgiving after Holy Communion such as: Let us pray with confidence for an increase of priestly and religious vocations as we remember in prayer:

Priests who have brought us the Sacraments.

Religious who have taught us and have now gone to God.

Priests and religious in purgatory and have no one to pray for them.

The missioners in foreign lands who are serving for Christ.

The lay missioners who are giving of themselves.

The generous youth whom Christ is calling to serve Him.

The religious communities who need vocations to carry on their work.

The dioceses that need an increase in priestly vocations to bring the Sacraments to the people of God.

True Christian witnesses whose apostolic zeal will bring many souls to Christ.

The students here present that they will follow whatever vocation God calls them to.

The parents of students that they will encourage vocations as they develop within their families personal love for Christ.

Catholic educational leaders need to promote creative programs that will offset the secularism that is so destructive. Young adults must be trained to cope with the evils found in the world dominated by humanism and materialism. Immorality increases with the want of respect for life, abortion, violence, euthanasia, slums, prisons that are so inhuman, the disregard for marriage, the increase of divorce, and the decline of family life. Youth must play an active part in destroying these evil forces that prevent Christ's message from reaching His people.

Consecrated Religious and Priests

The seminar where the vocation of man was considered offered an excellent preparation for an understanding of the work of priests and religious and an appreciation of their way of life.

The study of the place of religious life is essential in this age of the laity. They must have an appreciation of these religious apostolates that they might encourage others, and in time their own children. They must pray for an increase of vocations during this time of crisis. Vocations come from prayer and sacrifice. Youth must be exposed to such programs that they will assume personal responsibility to see that God's work on earth will continue through the instruments He has chosen to fulfill His plan for men.

One of the effective ways to create a climate for understanding the generosity that enables one to give of self out of love to the service of others is to consider people who have. Offer students a concrete program, examples of consecrated lives. Here are two programs, and religious teachers will recommend others.

For the lower classmen, play the record of Tom Dooley after giving a brief account of this play-boy, social doctor from the United States. He returned to Laos, to his people. The sense of humor that Dr. Dooley portrays on his different records will hold youth as they come to admire this young doctor who has such love and compassion for neglected people.

Some students might choose to read books and articles giving an account of his work which they could report on as part of this vocation preparation. They might be motivated to volunteer their services through many of the opportunities encouraged in our schools as did the high school youth when Dr. Dooley lived. They presented programs that raised money, and collected medical supplies and soap for the sick people whom he cared for in Asia.

For the upper classmen, show the film entitled *Something Beautiful for God*, which gives an account of the work of Mother Theresa of Calcutta who gives herself completely to the service of God's poor, neglected, and dying people in the slums of India. Within the last two decades she has founded a religious community which has enjoyed remarkable growth as they dedicate their lives to suffering humanity. They see Christ in each soul they assist out of love.

To give these students an appreciation of religious life, spend some time on the words of Mother Theresa. Here are some of the thoughts Mother Theresa shared with a large crowd of laity at a recent convention that students could consider:

"To be a Christian, we must go out to others, to give of self, to make all people feel wanted, feel loved, and feel important for they are important. To do this, we must be real, genuine, not superficial. We must take time to listen, to really listen. This is acting Christ-like and we are called to be other Christs or why be?

Life needs love and sacrifice, great love for the poor. Poverty is being unwanted, unloved, uncared for. There are so many people we do not accept. Begin where you are, the people you meet every day. You do not have to go to distant lands to take care of the poor, the unwanted, the unloved. Smile at people. Say kind and encouraging words.

Give your life to Christ. Let Him take over; let Him have full possession of you and you will grow in love, in His love which you will give to others. The world is more hungry for love than for food today.

Reflect frequently on 'Jesus loves me'. Realize this concept of love and you will be able to give love to others; you will grow in love. If you really loved, you would not complain, you would not gripe.

The poor are rich in love, in gratitude, in appreciation of God's gifts. The poor never grumble or complain for they are other Christs. Touch the poor, go to the poor, work with the poor and you will touch Christ where He dwells. All Christ wanted when He walked the earth was peoples' love. He asked for it. He still asks for our love shared with others."

Religious are called to teach the ignorant as teachers, to work with the sick as nurses, to help the needy as social workers. These apostolates offer many forms of helping those who stand in need of our assistance. Religious are Christ's co-workers who must go out, reach out to those who need them.

To work with the poor in any form is a gift. Think of all those who hunger for love, are poor for want of love, are lonely, the old, those in convalescent homes, the children who are neglected by divorced parents, the sick in the hospitals, those in prison. What love do we give them? Are we apathetic, indifferent? Christ calls all Christians to go to them, to love them, to help them. No one else has to ask you.

People must see Jesus in each one of us in our compassion, our real concern, our true love. Fill the world with love. This is our mission. This is the way to change the world. They need our help more than our money for they want to learn how to help themselves. They come from God and have a right to live and die with dignity with the love that we can give them. Work with a vision. See Christ in every life.

As Mother Theresa continues in the explanation of the work of her community among the poor and neglected she recommends a life of prayer in this service for others and especially stresses devotion to the Eucharist, to the Rosary, and the Holy Hour:

"The secret of the growth of our community is from prayer. The love that we give Christ in the Blessed Sacrament through our daily hour of adoration enables Him to work in us. There we learn His love, how to love, and how to give love to His people. Christ left us Himself in the Eucharist so that we can continue to grow in His love.

Say your Rosary daily. As you meditate on each mystery you will see life and love at its fullest. He has called each one of us to love as He loves. Pray the Rosary so that many of the destructive evils that are growing will cease. Time spent before the Blessed Sacrament will enable us to grow in love, to bring Christ to the poor. Live face to face with Jesus as you pray in

His presence. Read Scripture and let Christ speak to you. He will.

The moral evils in the United States are much more serious, much more destructive than the miseries of poverty in Calcutta. The wealth of this nation will disappear completely for people do not know how to love and to love consistently."

This exhortation of Mother Theresa might set the stage for consideration of religious life. It also helps direct the thoughts of youth to the need for prayer and for loving service.

Additional inspirational lives of religious could be suggested for students to read during this study of call to discipleship such as any one of the following or others recommended by the teacher:

Mother Cabrini, foundress of a religious community and first American saint. Mother Seton, foundress of the first community in the United States and a Saint. Father Rice and Bishop James A. Walsh, founders of Maryknoll, American Missioner Community. Bishop Ford, American Missioner in China. Father Hecker of the Paulists in the United States. Father Pro, martyr in Mexico during the revolution.

While students are reading the books of their choice small groups could prepare panels that would enable the class to have an understanding of the commitment that Christians are called to make whether as a member of the laity or a religious community, especially now with the stress upon evangelization.

Catholic educators will offer programs that form students spiritually. Then they will become effective leaders in the varying fields of volunteer services. Many of them will choose to work in their parishes, in hospitals, in convalescent homes, among disturbed and handicapped children, to teach religion classes to public school students at different levels, to lead discussion groups, and to organize and participate in Scriptural prayer groups with other teenagers.

The involvement of youth in the works of Christ offers the

most effective vocational recruitment program that Catholic educators could sponsor. The place and value of religious life with the grace of God would encourage youth to consecrate their lives through religious vows in the apostolic works of the Church.

Apostolic Experiences

Ask students to select a panel on suggested chapters and decrees from Vatican II, on the lives of founders of religious communities recommending those founded after the reformation, those founded in the 19th century, those founded in the United States, and the newer types of religious communities that have been established.

Assign students different communities to interview if possible and to report on the apostolic works in which they are engaged. Include certain phases of religious life such as community life, prayer life. They might give an account of the founding of that community.

Locate slides or films about different communities and present the program to the class. Or have them invite communities that will present their own program and answer questions. Each year sponsor a different program, like communities that teach, that nurse, that work with the aged and poor, social service workers, missioners, lay missioners, members of lay institutes, etc.

Visit places where religious serve such as retreat houses, the homes for the aged, training centers for teachers, social workers, etc.

Keep a bulletin board during this time of study on religious vocations. Have students be responsible for changing each week. Give them ideas. Take pictures of same.

Hold a sacrifice-day once a week. Have students develop. Select these suggested practices that students will offer for an increase of vocations such as: Make a visit each day this week for missioners. Say certain prayers for an increase of priestly vocations, etc.

Ask students to select one day in the month that they would attend Mass and pray for vocations. The class would then be represented each day as the students pray. They could also include the intentions of their classmates at this monthly Mass.

Encourage creative students to make banners to use in chapel or in the classroom on particular themes such as: Christ loves me. Christ needs me, etc.

Ask students to choose one of the following and to read about their work, interview a member of the community, or write for information on each one. They will enjoy this activity:

Secular institutes and how they differ from the so-called religious congregations. Why do they differ in their Christian witness? Why are they larger in Europe than in America? *Opus Dei* as a form of religious institute that differs from those of a secular group. Report on their influence throughout the world. The different forms of Third Orders such as the Carmelites, the Franciscans, the Dominicans, and other auxiliaries connected with religious communities. Compare the rules of some of these with religious life today.

Explain the spiritual life of the following who have particular apostolates and yet must follow a certain rule: St. Vincent de Paul Society, the Theresians who work and pray for an increase of vocations, the Legion of Mary who care for people, the Serrans who encourage priestly vocations. Secure pamphlets that will describe their missions. Select communities of women and read their history, report on their apostolates and growth. Visit a place they are involved in as part of their apostolate. Try to visit places that differ from teaching and nursing. Consider communities that were founded especially in the United States during the 19th or 20th centuries and report on their purpose, their founder, and give an account of why they have enjoyed such rapid growth.

As the vocation program draws to a close, teachers could make a survey that might be helpful for planning future programs or for evaluating the effectiveness of this program. Make the questions brief, constructive, and positive.

An Interesting Thought

The publication you have just finished reading is part of the apostolic efforts of the Society of St. Paul of the American Province. A small, unique group of priests and brothers, the members of the Society of St. Paul propose to bring the message of Christ to men through the communications media while living the religious life.

If you know of a young man who might be interested in learning more about our life and mission, ask him to contact the Vocation Office in care of ALBA HOUSE, at 2187 Victory Blvd., Staten Island, New York 10314. Full information will be sent without cost or obligation. You may be instrumental in helping a young man to find his vocation in life. *An interesting thought.*